"*Starting on Monday*, taken seriously by laborers and CEO's alike, could restore moral credibility to the workaday world."

Chicago Catholic

"A unique book ... [with] how-tos that teach and instruct seekers in do-able ways to live Christian lives in that most demanding location, the workplace."

Chicago Messenger

STARTING ON MONDAY

Christian Living in the Workplace

Rev. William P. Mahedy
Christopher Carstens, Ph.D.

BALLANTINE BOOKS • NEW YORK

Grateful acknowledgment is made to each of the following for
permission to reprint previously published material:

Doubleday & Company, Inc. and Darton Longman & Todd,
Ltd: scripture quotations from *The Jerusalem Bible*. Copyright
© 1966, 1967, 1968 by Darton, Longman & Todd, Ltd. &
Doubleday & Co., Inc. Reprinted by permission of the
publishers.

Moody Press: the appendix to *Nave's Topical Bible* by Orville
Nave, Moody Press edition, Moody Bible Institute of Chicago.
Used by permission.

Library of Congress Catalog Card Number: 86-47849

ISBN 0-345-36457-0

Manufactured in the United States of America

First Ballantine Books/Epiphany Hardcover Edition: June 1987
First Mass Market Edition: February 1990

This book is dedicated, with love, to our families—Carol, Michael and Marie Mahedy, and Linda, Jessica, and Adrian Carstens.

We also dedicate it to our parents, William P. and Loretta Mahedy, and William and Jean Carstens.

Contents

Acknowledgments

We wish to thank those who contributed to this book. Linda Carstens carefully and incisively edited the manuscript before it was submitted. Our editor at Ballantine, Toni Simmons, has been supportive throughout the project, and our literary agent, Sandra Dijkstra, has been consistently helpful. Their contributions are greatly appreciated.

An Invitation

WELCOME TO *STARTING ON MONDAY: CHRISTIAN Living in the Workplace*, a book for people who want to do their jobs well and be faithful to the Gospel at the same time.

We spend more than half of our waking hours at work. But because Christians work at so many different jobs, each with its own special demands, it can appear that they have little in common. Yet vastly different jobs can present similar challenges to all of us who take religious commitment seriously. Throughout a lifetime of little decisions, many made at work, the big decisions are made about what sort of people we are.

This is really not a complex idea. For example, by responding to other people's needs and wants, even in small ways, you develop a pattern of concern and generosity, regardless of whether you are a carpenter or an investment banker. Similarly, by grabbing a little of the other person's property when given the chance, your pattern becomes one of greed and theft, whether you occasionally toss one of the company's machine tools in the back of your truck, use the computer to transfer a few extra dollars to your account, or pad a bill for services rendered. These small decisions are the bricks with which you build your moral dwelling.

Jesus spoke to the employers and employees of His own time, landowners and tenant farmers, merchants, soldiers, tax collecters, and shepherds. He spoke to these ordinary people in their own language, using images that they recognized. Just how His statements apply to people in the twentieth century, though, may seem less clear. His message can seem muddled today, two thousand years later, by our difficulty in translating His words and in relating to the lives of those first listeners.

Jesus gave us moral guidelines embedded in stories about lost sheep, buried treasures, and hand-planted seeds. Who knows anything about sheep these days? You might scratch your head and wonder, "What has this got to do with selling cellular telephones?" You may sincerely wish to live the Christian life at work, and still find it a challenge to figure out how to do it.

A Christian life does not consist of selling church raffle tickets to co-workers, proselytizing the sales staff, or slipping religious pamphlets into colleagues' mailboxes. It does not allow you to consider yourself superior to those who do not share your beliefs. Rather, it calls for consciously developing patterns of thinking, decision making, and action based on a personal experience of Jesus as He is met in the Scriptures, in prayer, and in your daily life.

Starting on Monday: Christian Living in the Workplace is meant to help you reflect on the moral value of your work and the decisions you make on the job. It is not a simplistic book—it does not contain an index of sins to avoid nor any "sure fire" roads to wealth, riches, and the pearly gates. Life presents hard moral questions, and some of them require careful thought and tough choices. On the other hand, this book is not a graduate-school ethics text of complex essays on ethical philosophy and theology. *Starting on Monday* is meant to be a practical guide for Christian decision making, and though it is not a workbook, it does include some very helpful exercises for developing awareness of moral questions and some step-by-step guides to direct your reflection and help you make more satisfying choices.

Finally, we do not present a "new morality." The ideas in this book are carefully drawn from centuries of traditional Christian moral thought based on the Gospels.

There is no need for a new approach to moral thinking—rather, Christians need to do more moral thinking using the approaches given us by our faith.

We see two major steps in Christian decision making. The first is preparation. "In your minds you must be the same as Christ Jesus," wrote the apostle Paul, and shaping the mind to be ever more like Christ is a lifetime task. The second step, choosing Christian action, requires a specific response to a specific situation. Across the years we develop patterns of virtuous thinking and action, but each new decision is tough since it must be made individually and usually with little time to think it over.

Jesus gave us two great commandments. The first is to love God with all our mind and heart. Our first book, *Right Here, Right Now*, offers spiritual exercises for making this commandment a present reality. *Starting on Monday* addresses the second great commandment, that we love our neighbors as ourselves. For the Christian, moral behavior is love made manifest. As you live the Gospel on the job, Christ's love becomes part of the very fabric of your life.

Everybody Wants Success, Whatever It Is

EVERYONE CRAVES SUCCESS. STORES ARE FILLED WITH books on how to dress for success, invest for success, pray for success, and use mental imagery to increase your success potential. Motivational speakers fly all over the country and are amply paid for sharing their secrets for achieving success. Advertisements offer success courses, articles report success stories, and sure-fire formulas for becoming successful abound. Success—whatever it is—appears to be of primary importance.

Yet success is a hard concept to define. If you stood outside an auditorium and polled people entering a seminar on "The True Meaning of Success" you would be able to jot down many different definitions—there would be no shortage of opinions! However, you might not hear one that matched your own idea of success.

The following is the first of a number of exercises which will ask you to stop and think about a question or take time to write down your thoughts on an idea before continuing with the text. It is best to do these exercises immediately, as they are presented. Each is designed to help you learn about yourself, bring about some new awareness, or help you try out a new way of thinking about a problem. You can gain much more from this book by doing the exercises as soon as they are given. The reading will take longer, but it will be well worth the time spent.

Exercise #1: What Would Success Be for You?

Suppose for a moment that there really were a sure-fire formula for success, a simple thirty-second gimmick that would make you magically successful. This gimmick, practiced five times a week, would guarantee you success at any enterprise you chose, in six months or less. Imagine that you have been taught this technique. What sort of success would you choose? Take a minute to think about what professional success would mean to you. How would you know that you were successful? What signs would prove your success?

Take a minute to do this exercise before you read on.

No two readers will have exactly the same response to this exercise; everyone has individual hopes and dreams. However, because of a common set of cultural standards, people often have similar ideas about success. We present various typical measures of success in the remainder of this chapter. Even if a standard is not your own, try to notice ways in which you may have come to accept it nonetheless.

The first common standard for judging success is numerical. Americans love numbers and we often use statistics to define success. Some ventures lend themselves to numerical evaluation. For example, a professional baseball player who bats .320 with twenty-six home runs is a much better batsman than his teammate who bats .228 and rarely gets a double. A typist who produces 110 error-free words per minute is doing a better typing job than one who types sixty words per minute and reaches constantly for the correction fluid. Insurance salespeople add up the total dollars in coverage sold and evaluate their efforts. The list goes on and on. Anybody can define success by choosing something measurable or countable.

Exercise #2: Looking at the Numbers

How do you measure your own success in numbers? At work do you judge yourself or do others judge you by a numerical standard? What totals would you like to achieve? What are the numbers others pressure you to reach?

Take a minute to think about your own numerical standards for success before reading on.

Defining success by this deceptively simple procedure is nothing more than deciding what to count and then counting it. However, as soon as one tabulation is started, someone else wants to count a different process, or insists that the crucial elements are not really quantifiable. Defining the criteria for success in terms of numbers leaves out the "intangibles." This is apparent even in that previously mentioned and very countable enterprise, baseball. A player may bat only .228, but if he wins games with his defense, he still does a lot for the team. The steady veteran who inspires the team under stress may be more successful than another player with a better batting average. The slower typist may be better at organizing the flow of office work, while the faster one may argue all day with the staff about their dictation. And, a salesman may have a big year personally but undercut so many colleagues that overall sales drop as people stop working together.

Many more examples could be given, but the conclusion remains the same. The attractive clarity of numerical standards often turns out to be an illusion due to factors, some of which are important human truths, not included in the calculations. This is not to say that numbers can never play a valuable role in defining success—they often do. It is rather that numbers, by themselves, can be unsatisfactory criteria. Easily quantified information is sometimes superficial, reflecting artificial judgments. Truly meaningful criteria often resist being jammed into numbered boxes.

A second commonly shared standard for judging success is promotion, "moving up the ladder." Success brings promotion, and promotion brings increased responsibility, additional influence, and extra income.

Exercise #3: Thinking About Promotions

Take a minute to think about promotions. If you were promoted tomorrow, what job would you have? What is the next step "up the ladder" for you? How would the promotion change your life? In what ways would your work life be better? In what ways might it be worse?

Now, think about some of the people you know who have been promoted. How were they chosen? Perhaps you can recall people who were given new responsibilities because of their outstanding work. Can you think of people who were promoted for other reasons?

Take a few minutes to think about promotions before you read on.

Promotion is a faulty standard for success. In most workplaces, only a fraction of the people can be promoted because there are so few upper-level jobs. By the "success equals promotion" standard, all of the people who are not promoted are automatically identified as failures, no matter how well they continue to perform their jobs.

7

The "success equals promotion" standard is especially insidious in the human service occupations—teaching, social work, youth counseling, medical technology—where large numbers of highly skilled people perform very demanding work, often with little chance for promotion. The likelihood that most people in such occupations will "move up the ladder" is small, because there are so few supervisory jobs. The "promotion equals success" standard is extremely disheartening for those who continue frontline human service. If they haven't moved into administration, they can feel like failures by definition, no matter how well they perform their vitally important work.

The final flaw in the "success equals promotion" standard is the well-known fact that promotions are often given for questionable reasons. People may be promoted because they enthusiastically and uncritically support every administrative direction, because they play tennis with the boss, or because they have mastered office politics and know how to manipulate the director. The person promoted may be the best worker, or the best-suited for the upper-level job, but this is certainly not the case every time. Any standard that categorizes most of the workers in any job as unsuccessful is inaccurate.

Another common way to judge success is visible wealth or possessions. The American Dream has become a shopping list, and we have accepted a material standard of success.

Exercise #4: Your Wish List

What are the things which you would like to own? Take a minute to think about the possessions you desire. If you were more successful, would you have more of them? Or, looking at it another way, if you had them, would you feel like more of a success?

Take a few minutes to consider your wish list before you read on.

It may seem that whoever has the next possession on your wish list is successful. If you have an old car, the neighbor with a new pickup looks successful. If you rent a nice apartment, the family in the new condo just drips with success. Those with no money envy those with bank accounts who in turn envy those with investment portfolios.

Possessions are a faulty standard, even from a totally secular point of view. First, possessions can be lost or stolen, or may simply wear out. Then something new is needed to bring back that feeling of success. Second, many people know men and women with great visible wealth who pay a terrible personal price to maintain the image of success.

One of the authors once met a man whose first action after being introduced was to flash a fat roll of bills in a gold money clip and begin promoting the business scheme that made him "rich." It turned out that he had lost over a hundred thousand dollars in a worthless pyramid scam. He had sacrificed his home and all his possessions, in a desperate attempt to become rich—to own the things which would make him a "success." The bills in the gold clip were the only money he had, and he used them to impress new prospects, to lure them into the same phony business which had left him too poor to buy groceries for his children.

Examples are numerous. Many people take second mortgages to buy thirty thousand dollar motor homes so as to impress their friends and relatives with the juggernaut in the driveway. More than one investment broker has ended up in jail after a spree of high living, during which investors' funds were illegally spent on a "successful" lifestyle. The success of another person cannot be judged by his possessions; there is no way of knowing what it cost to get them, what real needs went unmet to buy the visible trappings.

In the end, possessions cannot form the ultimate criterion for success, because there is always something newer, something better, something more rare and costly to desire. Possessions are not inherently satisfying. To prove this point, take the guided bus tour of the stars' homes in Beverly Hills. These people have achieved the ultimate in material success. They have elegant cars, multimillion-dollar homes, money to throw at whatever strikes their fancy. Even so, at any one time house after house in the area is being remodeled in some new and expensive way because the owners are not yet satisfied. And, as the well-versed tour guide is likely to point out, many homes are on the market because the occupants are divorcing and dividing up their property. If these people are successful, why are they so visibly dissatisfied with their lives?

A fourth common standard for judging success is the attainment of recognition, the admiration of others. Success, this standard holds, is in the eye of the beholder: when those around you admire your work or your attainments, you have reached a higher level of accomplishment.

Exercise #5: Recognition and Success

Recall a time someone recognized the quality of your work or some special accomplishment of yours. How did you feel? What was it like to be noticed in this special way?

Now, see if you can remember an occasion when someone whom you had admired—a personal acquaintance or a celebrity—was exposed in a scandal. Can you remember how you felt about that person? Can you recall the reactions of others?

We all have hidden flaws, secret sins which we hide from others. What would it be like if the people who admire you learned of your private defects? How would it change their opinion of you? Just how uncomfortable would you be?

Take a minute to think about admiration and its loss before continuing.

Accomplishment should be recognized and praised. The problem with admiration as a criterion for success is that it is almost always based on partial knowledge. We often admire people about whom we know very little, and the reality of their lives can be a sorry disappointment. In recent memory, presidents, bishops, wealthy businesspeople, and famous evangelists have all felt the cold blast of admiration turn to disdain. No one is immune. When people discover the human frailties of their chosen models of success and good living, adulation can quickly turn to anger, even feelings of betrayal.

When others admire you, they usually admire the person they want you to be, rather than the person you really are. We hide flaws and weaknesses as much as we can—even from ourselves—and only those closest can know the things we would rather keep covered. Admiration feels wonderful, but it is often attained by highlighting that which we want others to know, while pretending that our faults don't exist. Whenever those are uncovered, the people who admire the false image will turn away.

Before moving on, it must be pointed out that people who make their living in the church often use the same five faulty standards to judge their own success. Numbers are a typical standard for judging one's ministry. Just count how many come to the services or to the retreat, the seminar or the revival. Add those who watch the TV ministry, and it is easy to be convinced that the numbers are a direct measure of how well one is doing. However, getting people into a meeting hall or having them tune in a radio show may or may not mean that

11

they are embarking on a meaningful, long-term involvement with the church. They may just be enthusiastic visitors, and not part of the Body.

Similarly, workers in the church can get involved in the race for promotion. Who will get to be the bishop's secretary, who will be named to the national council, who will sit on the governing board? Surely the many ministers, priests, and lay people who are not bishops or lay directors cannot all be failures.

The church may fall into the competition to collect material possessions. Congregations build bigger buildings and buy newer buses. A minister may judge the success of his or her efforts by those additions made to the physical plant. And more than one cleric has diverted church funds to purchase a new personal car or to make extravagant improvements in the pastor's living quarters.

Finally, admiration comes easily to preachers and youth ministers. They also can become addicted to the thrill of recognition, and maintain it through subtle—and not so subtle—deception.

What is to be done? The standards which our society uses for defining success turn out to be unsatisfying. They describe a success which is an illusion, which falls apart on close examination. Church workers appear to be as susceptible as workers in secular fields. If none of this is real success, then what is?

The Christian answer is not comprised of a list of desirable attainments nor a set of guidelines for evaluation. The Christian answer is a person, Jesus of Nazareth. You can truly evaluate your success by only one standard: how well have you traveled on the path which He showed you? Are you following Jesus?

Jesus did not reject the real world. He did not demand that the landowners give up their land nor that the laborers work for nothing. He made it clear that they could—must—live out the Gospel in their working lives. You are also called to this journey. Whatever your job, whatever

12

your level of attainment, whatever degree of success you have achieved, the call is the same.

And he said to them, "Follow me . . . . " (Matthew 4:19)

• 2 •

Preparation and Choosing:
The Two Steps in
Christian Moral
Decision Making

CHRISTIAN LIFE IS A JOURNEY WITH JESUS. MORAL decision making entails discerning His direction—figuring out where He is leading—and choosing to go along with Him.

The basic decision to follow Jesus is neither simple nor automatic. Baptism does not turn people into holy robots; it does not mechanically redirect their hearts and minds. Everyone makes a number of choices every day, and some of these decisions are headaches. All of us would like our options to be straightforward but in the real world we often have to pick between alternatives that are less than perfect. The working lives of most men and women do not contain much black and white, only a lot of grey.

At this point, it would be handy to introduce some sure-fire formula for Christian decision making—a simple three- or four-step program that would cut through every difficult decision. It could be printed on a gold-edged index card and carried in your pocket or purse at all times. Unfortunately, no such formula exists.

14

Actually, that's not quite accurate. There is a formula for Christian decision making, and it could be written on a tiny slip of paper, although any apparent simplicity would be an illusion. Paul put the formula down in clear, concise language:

In your minds you must be the same as Christ Jesus. (Philippians 2:5)

Different translations use slightly different words, "Have this mind among yourselves, which you have in Jesus Christ. . . ," "Your attitude must be that of Christ," or "Let this mind be in you, which was also in Christ Jesus." Each translation carries the same message: learn how to think like Jesus. Christians are to consider their daily decisions in a special, Christ-like way.

But how do you learn to think like a Christian? The answer doesn't fit on a three-by-five card. Learning to think like a Christian is a long process that begins with superficial judgments and deepens into a profound identification with the person Jesus. Your mind becomes as His mind. This won't occur in a week or two but it can happen. And the process may resemble others you have already experienced.

A supervisor learns that an employee is making costly mistakes on one of the company's major accounts. Her initial angry impulse to "unload the clown" may be tempered by the knowledge that this particular "clown" is the sole source of income for a family of seven. Still, the company's owner has a legitimate right to expect protection from incompetent employees. A business may take years to build, but it can be ruined in a short amount of time.

Successfully dealing with this sort of problem, finding the best solutions for both employer and employee, requires a special ability, that of "thinking like a manager." The effective manager considers company and employee needs at the same time. No one is born with

15

this ability—it is acquired through experience and training.

Christians bear the additional responsibility of heeding the call of Jesus and considering His demands for the present moment of life. Those familiar with the New Testament know that Christ's standards are higher than those of most employers, yet just as one can learn to think like a manager, one can learn to think like a Christian.

Anyone who has labored through a high school or college ethics course may conclude that Christian moral decision making is an activity that only ministers, priests, and theologians can master. However, if only people with Ph.D.'s in ethics could follow Jesus, the Gospel would be of sadly limited value. Ordinary working Christian men and women—not just ethics professors and theologians—can indeed learn to think like Jesus.

You already know how to make decisions. In fact, most working people make very complex and challenging choices every day. Yet business decisions—"How can I keep down production costs?"—differ from ethical decisions—"How can I justly deal with my work force?"—because ethical choices are not based on easily quantified data, like profit and loss statements. They grow out of principles like truth, love, and mercy. If, though, you examine the decisions you now make successfully you will see that you can learn to make sound ethical choices as well. Let's set aside ethical questions for a while, and consider the practical, day-to-day decisions in your work.

Exercise #1: Difficult Decisions in Your Work Life

Think about the work you do for a living. What sort of day-to-day decisions do you make? What kind of choices are required by your work? Take as long as you need to recall a few of the practical problems you must regularly solve.

16

Think about the job-related decisions which you must regularly make before you read on.

Here are just a few examples of the difficult choices that working people confront in their jobs.

- An insurance underwriter assesses the needs of potential clients when proposing insurance programs. This entails helping the customers balance the benefits of full coverage against the costs of complete protection.
- Five phones ring at once, and the receptionist must decide which callers should be put on hold, which should be called back, and which should be put through immediately.
- The dairy farmer selects cows to breed. He carefully evaluates the amount of milk and butterfat produced by each animal and matches these characteristics to those of a number of available breeding partners. Each pairing of cow to bull can affect the herd's productivity for years to come.
- An attorney selects witnesses before taking a case to trial. He must consider whether a witness with important information may also introduce side issues that could lead to months of additional litigation and push settlement even further out of reach.
- In addition to the regular curriculum of reading, math, and social studies, elementary school teachers often find themselves required to teach any number of district or state mandated programs such as human relations, health awareness, and drug abuse prevention. Teachers must decide what to teach and when to teach it, all the while working within the limits of the school day and the children's ability to absorb information.
- The landscape designer finds workable compromises between the lush fantasy of the homeowner and the reality of the soil and terrain of the building site.
- A manufacturing line supervisor regularly solves problems involving complex machine tools. Stopping the assembly line for even five minutes can be remarkably

expensive, and the supervisor is under a great deal of pressure to make rapid, accurate decisions.

- A contractor estimating a job's cost must consider the needs of dozens of different suppliers, subcontractors, and groups of laborers—as well as his own need for a profit.

Working people are called upon daily to make decisions. The first few times you make any new decision, it is a strenuous task, but it becomes less so with time. Everyday choices on the job are manageable because you are used to making them. Certainly you make more competent decisions than would someone who walked in, unprepared, from the street. You have learned ways of thinking that a newcomer could not possibly know.

Exercise #2: Tough Decisions Other People Make All the Time

Take a minute and think about the decisions other people make every day. Just above was a sampling of choices people make on their jobs. Look back at that list and find a job unlike your own. Then imagine going to work and facing a problem right away, without preparation.

For example, if you work in a medical office, imagine coming up with a reasonable estimate for the immediate construction of a two-car garage by noon tomorrow. If your job is selling switchboard equipment, imagine teaching thirty-three five-year-olds reading in the morning and arithmetic in the afternoon. How would you begin? Could you possibly get it done right? Let yourself really consider what tomorrow would be like making *somebody else's* decisions. What would you do?

Spend a while thinking about somebody else's decisions before you read on.

You may not be able to solve another person's problems because you don't know how to evaluate them. Someone

18

with more experience might be able to give you advice and walk you through the process of solving them, but you could hardly do so alone. There is no alternative to adequate preparation.

Christian moral decisions, whether made at work or elsewhere, involve a two-step process. The first, preparation—learning to think like a Christian—is a lifelong undertaking. The second step—choosing Christian action—is a faster process, because working life demands concrete action. You cannot wait forever to decide.

Consider the first step of preparation. Every job requires training and skill, yet the more complex jobs require more sophisticated training and greater development of ability. Simple manufacturing jobs may be learned in a few days or weeks, while more professional or technical work takes years of study and training. You make your job decisions well, in part, because you have spent a long time preparing to do so.

Exercise #3: Think About the Preparation Needed to Do Your Own Job Well

How much time did you put into learning the job you have right now? Did you finish high school or take special courses in college or technical school? Did you complete an apprenticeship or undergo special training at work? If you were promoted to your current position, you probably spent months or years working at lower-level jobs before you were ready for your present responsibilities.

Think about the preparation you needed for your current job before you read on.

When you have worked at a job for a long time, the skills you use every day become second nature to you. Having mastered a certain way of thinking, you don't even notice it anymore. However, much of what experienced workers use is not common sense, or second nature, at all—it is

19

knowledge and skill acquired through training, practice, and hard work.

Preparation and experience change your perspective and adjust your thinking to a new outlook. Solutions come immediately to mind because almost any new problem resembles another, one successfully managed earlier. Christian decision making also requires preparation. Christian conduct grows out of a mind trained in thinking like Jesus.

Learning to think like a Christian is a developmental process. We have identified seven components, each of which helps to develop "that mind . . . which was also in Christ Jesus":

Component 1   Accept responsibility for making the decision yourself.

Component 2   Remember that you are in the presence of God as you make your decision.

Component 3   Remember your neighbor, and your responsibility to serve.

Component 4   Apply reason and experience.

Component 5   Look for direction in Scripture.

Component 6   Seek guidance from the church.

Component 7   Open the decision to God in prayer.

Each of the next seven chapters will provide practical guidance for examining these components.

The second step of decision making, choosing Christian action, can be made almost instantaneously. Often decisions are made rapidly, almost without an awareness that they have been made at all. A need arises, a responding action is taken, and work continues. While some decisions are reached this way, with little or no reflection, others are worried over for weeks. Even in those cases, though, the final choice of action often occurs quickly, when some new piece of the puzzle completes the picture. Either way, the decision is both the fruit of gradual preparation and a separate, immediate creative act.

Exercise #4: Recall a Time You Chose Action

Think about the most recent day you spent at work. Now, recall some decision you made in the last fifteen minutes of the work day. Maybe you decided to put off some dictation until the next day, or you decided to stay a few minutes late to finish it up. It might be that you chose to send a customer's complaint along to another department or to leave the lights on overnight for your plants. Pause for a moment, and recall a decision you made just before coming home from work.

Now, think about the act of selecting that particular course of action. How did you decide on it? What factors did you consider? This is not a time for dwelling on what you *should have considered*—just be honest with yourself. How did you actually make that decision?

Spend a moment reflecting on your decision-making process before you read on.

The act of deciding, even in a quick determination, can be surprisingly complex. Each decision can have many levels of issues, and people may choose better options if they are conscious of this. Preparation can help, but lots of us fall into sloppy habits, ignoring facts we ought to consider. Choosing the right action requires careful—even if rapid—attention to the most important issues.

Exercise #5: Think About Factors Which You Might Have Considered

Go back to the decision made just before going home. Spend a minute or two thinking about the factors you might have considered in your choice. What other people were affected by your action?

How would a long-term pattern of similar decisions, whether good or bad, affect your own work future?

If you had considered these factors before you came home from work, might you have chosen differently.

Spend a minute or two considering some factors which you may have ignored.

It is true that if you thought of all the possible ramifications of every action, you would accomplish very little. You would be frozen in a ponderous state of doubt and risk being fired for your inefficiency. Good decisions are made when the most important factors are considered, and poor ones occur when those important factors are not included in the process. Anyone who recalls a decision which turned out badly can attest to this. As soon as problems begin showing up, one becomes painfully aware of the variables which should have been thought of in advance.

Christianity demands the examination of factors beyond personal success and beyond one's own immediate well-being. Christian decisions are made in the light of the Gospel and within Jesus' view of who we are and how we should live our lives. One who hopes to decide well must be prepared to think about the call of Jesus in the moment of choosing action.

Saint Paul states the call to discipleship clearly:

Try, then, to imitate God, as children of his that he loves, and follow Christ by loving as he loved you, giving himself up in our place as a fragrant offering and a sacrifice to God. (Ephesians 5:1–2)

He then continues, amplifying the call by stating

You were darkness once, but now you are light; be like children of light, for the effects of the light are

22

seen in complete goodness and right living and truth. Try to discover what the Lord wants of you, having nothing to do with the futile works of darkness but exposing them by contrast. (Ephesians 5:8–11)

Truly Christian decisions require preparation—your mind must be "trained by practice to distinguish between good and bad." (Hebrews 5:14) And when choosing an action, the guiding principle should be the Gospel of Jesus, the light of faith. Jesus assures us that He will always be with us. It is our opportunity—and our responsibility—to remain close to Him on the journey.

3

Learning to Think
Like a Christian:
Component One—
Accepting Responsibility for
Making the Decision Yourself

A FAVORITE OLD HYMN SAYS IT SO CLEARLY—"I have decided to follow Jesus." That one great choice sets the standard by which all other decisions are measured. But all those other decisions still need to be made, one at a time, and you have to make them for yourself.

There would be no reason to devote an entire chapter to the need to accept the responsibility to decide if there weren't so many ways to avoid it, and if the results of indecision weren't so damaging to moral life. We have previously pointed out that ethical decision making is an acquired skill. An important part of that skill is accepting the fact that people really have to make their own choices.

Acceptance is not as simple as it might first appear. Letting someone else make the choices grants one a tempting illusion of safety. The person who convinces himself that someone else is responsible can avoid feeling guilty when the effects of the decision are negative. The one who decides bears the burden.

Yet you cannot really let somebody else decide, even

if that's what you'd like to do. You always decide for yourself. If someone else gives you instructions, you choose to follow them. Blind habit and comformity are choices. It is not possible to avoid decisions—there are only ways to *pretend* that you don't have to make them. Sadly, these ways seem especially common on the job.

People convince themselves that they are not responsible for their choices in a number of different ways. Few people can boast that they never blame somebody else for their actions. However, when the excuses are examined carefully, they always fall apart.

Handy Excuse #1: *"It's not my decision—my boss tells me what to do."*

This is the civilian equivalent of "I was only following orders." Most people work under a superior, and the excuse springs from the common belief that most employees have only limited decision-making opportunity. However, that belief is false, and even if it were true, it wouldn't completely remove the responsibility for commitment to action.

Some highly routine jobs, such as assembly line manufacturing, demand that each employee proceed in a very specific pattern, staying in lockstep with the other workers. The tempo is set by the machines, and the people work along in time. Those workers may actually have few options on the job, although they inevitably make some choices of their own.

For even in highly routine work, decisions are an everyday occurrence. Phone solicitors may work in a room with twenty other phone salespeople. The job in a "boiler room" is highly patterned—every word of the sales pitch is carefully memorized in advance. In such a setting, though, workers choose their level of relationship with fellow employees and their attitudes toward the people being called.

Most employees handle their own decisions as they do their jobs. Salespeople have quotas to meet, but they have a good deal of latitude as to how they get the orders on the books. Nurses, personnel clerks, and office managers are required to follow company policy guidelines, yet they are usually allowed some flexibility in interpretation, even in the most detailed book of work rules.

Ultimately, the boss can't be responsible for your decisions because you always have the option of leaving the job. Quitting is rarely a trivial decision, and can be terribly stressful, especially if you don't have another job lined up. But you always hold the final card. There are other jobs, and if an employer insists on your doing something that is clearly wrong, you can and must say "no"—and walk out the door.

Exercise in Recognition #1: You and Your Boss

Has an employer ever directed you to do something that you truly believed was immoral or wrong? More than one agency administrator has turned in travel vouchers for personal meals or travel, expecting the bookkeeper to put them through as business expenses. In other cases, one may be pressed to hire an influential politician's nephew, even though more qualified applicants are available. For this exercise the important issue is that you believed the action was improper when you were asked to do it.

What was the request, and what did you do about it? Did you balk at the request, or go along without protest? Was another choice available?

If such a time comes to mind, take a moment to relive that experience. What was it like?

Before you read on, take a minute to remember a time you were instructed to do something you thought was wrong.

It can be painful to say no to a supervisor who is pushing for something you don't want to do—it can even cost you your job. Many of us carry deep regrets for actions we took because the boss told us to. And when we recall those times of decision, we know we could have made different choices—the decisions were really ours. The excuse works for a time, but it breaks down upon close examination.

Handy Excuse #2: " *It's not my decision—they've always done things this way.* "

This is a disguised version of the first excuse, but with the blame placed on "them." What a comfortable way out—you aren't making any moral decisions because this is what has "always" been done! This excuse has another translation with the same meaning: "Everybody else is doing it."

The effect of either variation is to transfer the uncomfortable responsibility for your demanding decisions to someone else's shoulders. Behind this action lies a long and sorry history of sloppy morality. Employees who help their company pad customers' bills by filling out phony time sheets pretend that they aren't responsible because "they've always done it that way." And the kid who gets caught stealing from his employer at the carnival has a ready answer—"It's just like part of your pay. Everybody does it."

Major scandals have recently brought to light companies hiding multimillion-dollar defense contract overcharges by fancy bookkeeping. Other firms regularly drive up their profits by scaring trusting people into purchasing expensive services they don't need. Similarly, more than one physician has billed an insurance company for procedures that were not actually performed. Within those organizations, someone actually manipulates the books, closes the sales, and signs the insurance forms. People continue such actions, in part, because they convince themselves that it is an accepted way of doing business. "They've always done it that way. Everybody else is doing it."

Jesus reserved His strongest condemnations for people

27

who observe traditions but ignore the deeper duties of morality.

> And why do you, he answered, break away from the commandments of God for the sake of your tradition? (Matthew 15:3)

The Pharisees were the masters of "They've always done it that way." Jesus called them hypocrites, "whitewashed tombs that look handsome on the outside, but inside are full of dead men's bones and every kind of corruption." (Matthew 23:27) He explicitly discredited the contention that you can escape accountability by doing what everyone else does.

Exercise in Recognition #2: Just Who Are "They"?

Anyone who has ever worked for a company or agency with more than three employees has certainly run into "organizational habits"—ways of doing things which are accepted practices, whether or not they are efficient, cause ethical problems, or are just plain crooked. People keep doing things because they "have always done it that way."

You probably can come up with your own examples of things done in your office in an inhumane or deceitful manner because nobody actively opposed them. People talked about it in the lounge, but the practice continued. Maybe you were even involved.

Who told you to do it? Where did the directives come from? Sometimes there are explicit instructions, and sometimes people just follow an unspoken, but powerful tradition. Try to recall the source of those decisions.

If an example comes to mind, you must have sensed at the time that something was wrong. Otherwise you wouldn't have noticed the problem! How did you handle your uneasy feelings?

Before you read on, take a moment to recall a time when you recognized an organizational bad habit.

There have probably been times in your work life when you have stood up and said, "This is the wrong way to do things." Almost as surely, there have probably been times when you carefully avoided thinking about office conduct, or decided that going against the grain would cost too much. When you decided to agree to what "they" have always done you became one of "them." The choice not to oppose the action was your *own*. The blame for options you selected yourself cannot be transferred to others.

Handy Excuse #3: *"It's not my decision. I'm just a low-level employee around here, and what I do doesn't make much difference."*

This excuse is about power. People who don't have enough power to influence how things are done can't possibly be responsible for any problems that arise. How could just one individual among so many really make a difference?

Here again, there is some mental sleight of hand going on. As if by magic, you are able to disappear into the smallness of your position. You decide that you are powerless and—Presto!—the problems are no longer yours. If a carpenter notices that his fellow employees are systematically stealing tools from the company, he is in a bind; he is worried about the theft, but he does not want to be disloyal to his peers. By reminding himself of his powerlessness, he thinks, "Why say anything if it won't do any good? Nobody would listen to me. The foreman will have to do something about it." Thus the carpenter's problem is solved.

Suppose an engineer who works for a small company that is struggling to meet the delivery date on an important contract notices a tiny but potentially serious design flaw in the parts they are making. Should she call the chief engineer and tell him that they have to be redesigned? Should she keep her mouth shut and hope that the defect won't cause problems for the customer? Why should she call it to anyone's attention, if they won't listen anyway? "I'm not a design engineer, those guys have been here twelve years. They're not going to pay attention to what I say." Once again, hiding in smallness provides a way out of the bind.

Exercise in Recognition #3: Remembering Little People Who Made a Difference

Can one person really make a difference? Of course! The challenge is in recognizing an individual's potential for causing change.

All school children can name a few men and women who changed the world: George Washington, Einstein, Alexander the Great, Gandhi, Madame Curie, Martin Luther King, the Wright brothers, among others. Their actions in politics, religion, and technology produced changes which still make a difference in the way we live our lives—for good or ill. But brilliant scientists, leaders of nations, prophets and conquerors are not the only ones whose actions are meaningful.

Think about your personal history. Can you remember an individual whose actions changed the course of your life? Perhaps a teacher, an influential supervisor, or another worker said or did something which altered your direction in some important way. Can you recall a person whose actions made working conditions better for an entire group of employees? Or a co-worker who used his or her energy to make everyone else miserable by repeatedly disrupting other people's efforts?

Now try to recognize your own influence. Can you remember something you did that made an important difference to *even one* other individual? Did you ever help a friend find a job, or give important advice to a co-worker? Can you recall a time you took someone to lunch to tell him privately that he needed to clean up his act at the office? Did you ever help two fellow employees make peace after their anger had driven them apart?

Before you read on, take a moment to reflect on little people—including yourself—who have made a difference.

Having done it even once, you could do it again. Handy Excuse #3 doesn't hold up any better than the first two. You may control neither the company nor the world, but you are not powerless.

Handy Excuse #4: *"This may be my decision—and I know what I should do—but it would cost too much."*

Handy Excuse #4 is different than the others. This excuse pops up when the decision is clearly yours but you don't want to make it. This excuse is rooted in fear. Nobody wants to be humiliated, friendless, passed over for promotion or fired. Sometimes the correct moral decision can be perfectly clear but frightening because of its potential cost.

On rare occasions a moral decision can actually claim one's life. A recent military regime in Latin America detained, tortured, and murdered hundreds of civilians in camps located near busy residential neighborhoods. Many of the residents of those neighborhoods knew what was happening, but chose to be silent, lest the police squads appear at their doors. It is dreadful to face a moral decision which may endanger your life or the lives of your children. Not everyone can hope to be a hero in the face of raw terror.

Fortunately, there are few life-and-death decisions waiting for most people at work tomorrow. Nonetheless we frequently invoke the "it would cost too much" excuse for decisions where the actual risk is nowhere near so high. We all fear being embarrassed or inconvenienced, and many working men and women compromise their moral principles because they don't want to

31

be made the butt of a joke. More than one ambitious member of a firm has kept his or her mouth shut because "they only promote team players around here." It is one thing to go along with immoral practices because objecting to them would bring the death squads to your door, and quite another to do so because protest might keep you from becoming sales manager.

Fear is a powerful motivator. It is unfair to sit in judgment of another's situation, to think that the other's fear is inconsequential. You may lack sympathy for those who find rejection the most terrifying of experiences if you yourself are not afraid of it. Be careful not to judge others harshly. And, it is important to remember that the only way you can get past your own personal fears is to stop running from them long enough to examine them carefully. They may not be as frightening as they seem.

Exercise in Recognition #4: What Is the Price of Your Ethics?

This exercise may be painful, because it requires you to acknowledge a situation of failing to live up to your own standards. Try to recall a time at work when you knowingly did something wrong because you were pressed by fear of the consequences of doing the right thing. One woman went along with some office gossip because she didn't want to be considered unfriendly or "too holy." An IRS agent closed his eyes to petty embezzlement because he feared the reaction of those involved.

Something may leap to mind, or you may need to reflect for a while. Take however long you need to recall a time when you made the wrong ethical decision out of fear.

People fear numerous things: a dreaded loss of promotion, humiliations, or transfer to a less desirable work area. What did you fear when you fell short of your personal expectations? Now, take a good look at what you were afraid of. How bad would it actually have been if it had come to pass? The only way to overcome a fear and to find out if it is really deadly is to face it. Is it possible that you let a small anxiety dictate your ethical behavior?

Before you read on, reflect on a time you let fear set the price of your ethics.

The Gospel makes it quite clear that men and women are responsible for their own choices and that excuses do not diminish that responsibility. Jesus made this particularly clear in the parable of the invited guests.

> There was a man who gave a great banquet, and he invited a large number of people. When the time for the banquet came, he sent his servant to say to those who had been invited, "Come along: everything is ready now." But all alike started to make excuses. The first said, "I have bought a piece of land and must go and see it. Please accept my apologies." Another said, "I have bought five yoke of oxen and am on my way to try them out. Please accept my apologies." Yet another said, "I have just got married and so am unable to come."
>
> The servant returned and reported this to his master. Then the householder, in a rage, said to his servant, "Go out quickly into the streets and alleys of the town and bring in here the poor, the crippled, the blind and the lame." "Sir," said the servant "your orders have been carried out and there is still room." Then the master said to his servant, "Go to the open roads and the hedgerows and force people to come in and make sure my house is full; because, I tell you, not one of those who were invited shall have a taste of my banquet." (Luke 14:16–24)

This parable contains many levels of meaning. Nonetheless, the obvious message is definite and valid: excuses are not acceptable, and do not relieve people of their accountability. The choice is still there.

The second step to recognizing your decisions is learning to notice them when you make them. When you hurry past decisions without reflection, your selections are usually not well formed. In fact, the ordinary excuses aren't even necessary if you are not aware that decisions are being made. You can make dozens of decisions in the course of the day and yet feel that you haven't decided anything at all.

The decisions will still be made, though, and they will be your decisions. However, they will be made by the unexamined forces of habit and conformity. Decisions made without consideration are made on impulse, and impulses do not produce the best actions. Decisions must be *noticed* as they are made. This is a discipline which requires practice and commitment. However, there are some exercises that can increase your awareness of decisions as they whiz by in your mind.

The first is a very simple exercise. Try it for ten minutes or so. You may want to repeat it from time to time because it strengthens the habit of recognizing your decisions *as you make them.*

Exercise in Recognition #5: Talk to Yourself About Your Decisions

Mentally label decisions as you make them. Even if you don't spend a lot of time pondering a decision, it will receive more attention if you simply acknowledge that you are making a choice. Let the decision register in your mind, and give it a name.

The exercise is simplicity itself. As a decision is being made, say silently in your mind, "Right now I am deciding to . . ." or "Right now I'm choosing to . . ." and finish the sentence. The mental monologue will then be filled with sentences like these:

- "Right now I'm deciding to mail this catalogue first class instead of catalogue rate."
- "Right now I'm choosing to call this client back right away."

34

- "Right now I'm choosing to ignore this memo and go ahead with my plan."
- "Right now I'm deciding to write to the plant manager about the problem with the pressure valves."
- "Right now I'm deciding to have a cup of coffee before I go to work on that roof."

This exercise leads to awareness of decisions as they are made. It also makes you aware of the frequency of daily options.

It would be frustrating to continue this exercise for longer than ten or fifteen minutes. You can try it a few times at work over the next several days, and come back to it again in the future. There is surprising depth in this simplest of strategies and more potential than shows on the surface. Try it and see what emerges.

Exercise in Recognition #6: Placing Reminders at Important Points for Decision Making

In each of our work lives, predictable periods of decision making occur, times when choices are called for more frequently. Common occasions for decision making include:

Meeting a new customer.
Placing an order with the supply house.
Picking up your telephone messages.
Beginning a new lesson or series of lessons.
Writing specifications for a job.
Reviewing the file of a client.
Going to the weekly staff meeting.
Talking to a union representative.
Meeting a new applicant.
Going over the books with the accountant.
Opening your mail.
Making an appointment book entry.
Discussing a contract with a customer.

Every job has its own periods for decision making. Go over your work day, briefly, and try to identify those times when a large number of decisions are called for.

Now think of a reminder, something to call attention to the decisions being made at those important points. One sales rep put a green sticker on her telephone as a reminder to consider her decisions while placing telephone calls. A large paper clip on the mail box helped another office worker recognize the need for decisions which his mail brings. A city council member put a tiny cross on the cover of her appointment book to remind her that decisions are required whenever she opens the book.

Plan on changing your signals from time to time because after a few days, the old signal will blend into the background. That's all right, because the most important reminder is the habit which develops in your thinking. The exercise is only a tool—and a time-limited one at that.

To agree to decide for oneself is a great challenge. The Christian must face that trial squarely and with courage. As the next chapters will show, our faith and tradition give us many tools for the demanding moments of moral decision making. We are called to follow Jesus, and there are plenty of signs to show us the way.

4

Learning to Think Like a Christian: Component Two— Remembering that Jesus Is with You on the Job

I T IS FRUSTRATING TO WANT TO FOLLOW JESUS, yet not be ready to give up the all-out hunt for success. Some people try to slip past this dilemma by drawing a mental fence around their work lives and dividing themselves into two parts. One part is for Jesus and the other is for pursuing wealth—and Jesus isn't supposed to interfere with the time devoted to being successful.

Jesus seems to fit in better on the weekend. Weekends are for home and family, for love and warm, caring times—and for going to church. Home and church are considered the right places for religion. People look to religion for inner peace and sustenance and for the feelings nurtured in family and friendship, intimacy, and sharing. You are probably more comfortable letting Jesus share your life at home and in the church.

But work is different. Americans, including many religious Americans, believe it is better to forget about all that "soft" stuff while at work. Work is about success, about toughness and competition. To be a Christian at work can be inconvenient. Therein lies the usefulness of the mental fence around your work. It lets you do what you want on the job by pretending that your actions don't affect your relationship with God. "After all," you may say to yourself, "He gets the whole weekend."

Jesus certainly would have considered such a compartmentalization an outright fraud. He had a great deal to say about work. In fact, He talked more about working life than about family life—and He never said anything at all about going to church on Sunday. After the love of God, nothing appears to have been more central to Jesus than working life.

Jesus used parables and images drawn from daily working life in Galilee. He spoke of sheep and shepherds, of workers and vineyard owners, of fishermen and day laborers. He discussed economic issues, ranging from lost coins to taxation. The life and teaching of Jesus did not advocate escaping the realities of everyday life and the working world. For Jesus, the kingdom of God began right in the midst of human life—and in the midst of the earthiest of all enterprises, earning a living.

So, if there is a line around your work life, remember that you put it there, not Jesus. If you want to conduct your work life in a Christian context, you'll have to rub out that line. You must invite Jesus onto the job.

Doesn't it seem a bit odd to think of inviting Jesus to go to work with you? Isn't He already there? Aren't we taught from childhood that God is everywhere? The church is called ". . . the fullness of him who fills the whole creation." (Ephesians 1:23)

Nonetheless, you must actively invite Jesus to your job for two reasons. First, if mental barriers are keeping Christianity out of your work life, it is because you built them, and you must work at tearing them down. Second, Jesus enters and redeems the world through the activity

38

of His followers. When you remember His presence and go out of your way to respond to His grace, you become His point of entry. He enters your office, factory, paintshop, or pressroom through you.

Exercise in Remembering #1: The Invitation

How might you invite Jesus into your workplace? Any small action, invisible to anyone but you, may be considered an invitation. You could make a note on your "to do" list, or say a special prayer on your coffee break. Or, you could put a Bible in your desk or a statue of St. Joseph on your bookshelf. You could bring a calendar from church and hang it in the shop, or find some special marker for the dashboard of your truck. Maybe you could turn off the car radio, and pray on the way to work.

There must be a hundred different ways of saying, "Be with me, Jesus." A simple action begins the process of inviting Him to join you at work.

Before you read on, reflect a moment on an act that might make clear your intention to invite Jesus to your job.

If you invite Jesus, He will surely respond. His presence—felt, known, and experienced by you—will change how you look at your work. You will see the world through different eyes, through eyes like His.

An invitation is only the beginning. A guest can be invited, only to be ignored all evening long. You can open the door for Jesus, and then promptly forget that you let Him in.

It is not unusual to forget everything but the job you're doing. There is always work to be done, and it can be pressing. Someone is bound to get upset with you if you don't get the job done. On the other hand, if you forget

39

the presence of Jesus, nobody but you will ever notice. Virtually any job will give you a lot more feedback on the quality of your work than on the quality of your spiritual life. Jesus doesn't fit in when the deadlines have to be met. The orders need to go out, the time sheets have to be recorded, and those tasks demand your attention. So your first invitation is likely to get washed away by the stream of business unless you go beyond those early good intentions.

The habit of remembering the presence of Jesus is the starting point for enhancing your Christian spiritual and ethical life "in the marketplace." It is also the ultimate goal. The closer you come to the goal of always remembering His presence, the closer you come to the total transformation of your life.

Jesus plainly said that He would be with us. The promise of His presence is evident in the Gospels.

And know that I am with you always; yes, to the end of time. (Matthew 28:20)

I will not leave you orphans;
I will come back to you.
In a short time the world will no longer see me;
but you will see me,
because I live and you will live. (John 14:18–19)

Your task is to actively bear His presence in mind. This has been called the Practice of the Presence of God. Constantly recalling that Jesus is with you is both the easiest and most demanding of all spiritual exercises. So it is probably best to start small, and let the awareness begin in a limited portion of your life. If given the chance, that awareness will spread.

Exercise in Remembering #2: Practicing the Presence of God

The best place to begin is right here and now. Take a moment to look up from your book and glance about the room. Remember that you are in the presence of God. *He really is here with you.*

What a remarkable notion! The Gospel says that Jesus is as present as the book you hold in your hand. Take a moment to let that reality sink in.

Now, mentally place yourself at work. Think about one of the things you do every day—waiting on customers, writing letters, talking to your supervisor—and imagine what it would be like to do that task with the knowledge that Jesus was *right there*. How might it change that moment of your day?

Before you read on, spend a moment thinking about how "Practicing the Presence of God" might change one moment of your next day at work.

The Practice of the Presence of God was first used by Brother Lawrence of the Resurrection, a French monk who found it almost impossible to pray in church. He discovered that he could be close to God at his work in the monastery kitchen.

Who hasn't heard someone say, "I feel closest to God in the mountains," or "When I sit and look at the waves on the lake, then I can really remember that I am with God." These are exemplary sentiments, except most people spend more time at work than at the beach or in the woods. Brother Lawrence experienced God's closeness as he made soup, bought vegetables, and carried out the kitchen scraps. That experience should be your goal, and it can be achieved if you remember that Jesus is with you at work, whatever you do for a living. Jesus, who was with Joseph in the carpenter's shop and with Peter in the fishing boats, prom-

41

ises to be with you wherever you work. You just need to remember that He's there.

So, just how are you to develop the habit of remembering the presence of God? It won't evolve by accident, or just because you think it is a good idea. Good intentions have a way of getting lost during busy times. A definite plan is necessary if you really want to become more open to God.

If you decide tomorrow to do every part of your job with a full awareness of God's presence, you will probably tire of and quit the exercise in thirty minutes. It is an unrealistic goal, especially if this is a new task for you.

Instead, pick an activity that you do at work several times each day. Your first choice might be a job that takes only a few seconds. The right activity for you might be picking up a telephone message, going to the back of the store for an item your customer can't find, or getting a particular tool out of your tool box. Begin with something rather routine and nondemanding. Practicing the Presence of God is a lot harder when you are under a lot of mental or emotional pressure, and you will be more satisfied if you start out with a relatively quiet, easy, and often repeated work task.

Whenever you do that single chosen activity next time at work, do it while *actively remembering* that you are in God's presence.

Exercise in Remembering #3: Thinking About Your Plan

Psychological research has shown that when you are learning to do something new it helps to imagine yourself doing it successfully. Right now, close your eyes and imagine that you are actually at work performing the task you have chosen for this exercise. Imagine yourself doing that task while actively recalling the presence of God. Take as long as you need to do this before you open your eyes to read on.

How did it feel to imagine yourself Practicing the Presence of God at work? If you imagined that again and again over days and weeks, how might it change your perception of work?

Spend a minute thinking about your plan before you read on.

Good intentions are often translated into action by following a plan. If you want to make the Practice of the Presence of God a part of your working life, make a point of following your plan of actively remembering that God is present whenever you do the task you have selected as your starting point.

Another way to make yourself at home with the idea of Jesus being present on your job is to imagine Him working with your tools. Our image of God is often that of a transcendant spiritual being rather than of an actual living being. But in Jesus, God stepped into the dirt and sweat of real human life. Be assured that He would be as comfortable in your work as He was in His father's carpentry shop.

Do the following exercise at work. It takes a few minutes, and requires some uninterrupted time. Try it on a coffee break.

Exercise in Remembering #4: Jesus Doing Your Job

Find a time when you can be quiet at work. The exercise can still be done even if total silence is impossible, but it will be more difficult. Begin by getting an unusual perspective on your work place. Position yourself five or ten feet away from where you work. If you usually sit, you might want to stand. If you are on your feet most of the time, you may consider sitting on the floor to do this exercise. You want to be "out of position" in the area where you work.

Take a look at the tools of your trade from this unusual point of view. You want to look at them with unfamiliar eyes, as though they belonged to someone else. When you work with something for months or years it becomes invisible. You want to try to see what your tools and your job surroundings really look like.

Imagine Jesus working with your tools. Try to see Him holding your pen, talking on your phone, using your drill press. Become a bystander and watch as He does your job. Take a few minutes to develop a sense of what it would be like to watch Jesus do your job. This may make some people feel incompetent. After all, it is easy to imagine that Jesus would do the job better than you. However, the purpose of this exercise is to accustom yourself to the thought that Jesus really did human work—work like yours.

During the next few days, try to find time to imagine Jesus working with your tools.

Saint Paul, in his first letter to the Corinthians, referred to Apollos and himself as "fellow workers with God." This has also been translated as "fellow workmen" and "co-workers" of God. The thought, "I am working on this project along with Jesus," has been repeated in so many tracts and sermons that it has become overly familiar and a cliché. How sad that is. One of the Gospel's most astonishing ideas is that individual humans can work alongside God to accomplish His ends. If you *really* think about that, it will make you dizzy. Why would God decide to work alongside people? We make so many mistakes. And yet the New Testament makes it clear that you are God's co-worker, as much as you are the co-worker of the other men and women on your job. Astounding!

Maybe it is too much to believe all at once. Such belief has to build slowly, steadily. One way to develop your sense of yourself as Christ's co-worker is to share your experiences with Him—in short, to talk with Jesus about your work.

You do that with your human co-workers all the time. Whenever two people work on a project together they almost inevitably end up discussing the job. A surprisingly powerful exercise is to simply talk over your work in prayer, out loud, as you might with a fellow employee. Talking to Jesus can remind you that you are on the job with Him. Find a moment when you can be alone—you don't want people thinking you're crazy, after all—and tell Him what's up.

Exercise in Remembering #5: Talking Shop with Jesus

Take a minute or so, right now, to talk out loud to Jesus about some project you are working on. There's no need to share your worst problem or ask for divine intervention. Rather, reflect a moment on what's happening on your job, and then simply *describe* to Him whatever comes to mind.

"Jesus, I'm trying to find a replacement for Harry. We're interviewing candidates, and it's confusing. They look pretty good, but how can I tell before they've really been on the job? Harry was a great help, and since he got promoted, it has been tough getting the work out. I sure hope we find someone who can do it."

Or your prayer might be, "Things are really looking up, Jesus. I wasn't sure we'd get that equipment loan, and it went right through the loan committee." You might find yourself saying, "This has been a really boring week. Nothing much going on at all—and I'm getting crabby for lack of something to do."

Before you read on, take a moment to talk shop with Jesus.

Sprinkle this exercise throughout your work day. Its goal is to erase the line around your work and to make you aware that He is with you as much as He is on the mountaintop or in the sanctuary.

Jesus chooses to walk beside you, even into the marketplace of twentieth-century America. Inviting Him to go there with you need not change the nature of your job nor the basic patterns of your day. But when you actually remember that you travel with Jesus in the workplace it will alter everything you do.

5

Learning to Think
Like a Christian:
Component Three—
Recognizing Your Neighbor
as a Real Person and
as a Child of God

THE VAST MAJORITY OF JOBS DEMAND INTERACTION with other people. Few can work completely alone and still make a living in the modern world. Gone are the days of the mountain man who hunted and trapped alone in the woods only to come out now and then for supplies. There may be a few of those positions around, but everybody else works in concert with others.

People come together to share work. Historically our ancestors first drew together in families and clans, and then formed villages, towns, and finally cities. Men and women have always worked together in groups, and the history of humanity is the story of larger and larger groups coming together to accomplish ever more complex tasks.

In the biblical story of creation, immediately after expulsion from Eden, Adam and Eve produce offspring and their children start sharing the workload. Only four chapters into Genesis, Abel becomes a shepherd and Cain tills the soil. The division of labor has begun. In the same chapter, Enoch founds the first town, and his descendents become herdsmen, musicians, and metalworkers. The labor is allocated among them, with each taking a part. Sharing work is so basic for men and women that God *punished* Cain by driving him from the community, to be a "fugitive and wanderer over the earth." (Genesis 4:12) To be human is to share labor—our ancestors knew that before they knew how to call on God by name. (Genesis 4:25)

Jesus often told stories about working men and women; many of His parables concerned employment. Central to these stories was the blending of two themes: the proper relationship between man and God and the proper relationship between man and his fellow man. Jesus said that morality made two basic demands, to love God and love your fellow man. A scribe once asked Jesus what was the greatest commandment, the most important rule to follow in life. His answer was very direct.

This is the first: Listen, Israel, the Lord our God is the one Lord, and you must love the Lord your God with all your heart, with all your soul, with all your mind and with all your strength. The second is this: You must love your neighbor as yourself. There is no commandment greater than these. (Mark 12:29-31)

As He approached the end of His life, Jesus again made the point at a supper with His followers. Calling them His little children, He placed upon them the demand of love.

I give you a new commandment:
love one another;
just as I have loved you,
you must love one another.
By this love you have for one another,
everyone will know that you are my disciples.
(John 13:34-35)

48

Even if it were only applied to fellow churchmen or close friends this would be a high standard to uphold. But Jesus pressed the issue even further.

> But I say this to you who are listening: Love your enemies, do good to those who hate you, bless those who curse you, pray for those who treat you badly. To the man who slaps you on one cheek, present the other cheek too; to the man who takes your cloak from you, do not refuse your tunic. Give to everyone who asks you, and do not ask for your property back from the man who robs you. Treat others as you would like them to treat you. If you love those who love you, what thanks can you expect? Even sinners love those who love them. And if you do good to those who do good to you, what thanks can you expect? For even sinners do that much. And if you lend to those from who you hope to receive, what thanks can you expect? Even sinners lend to sinners to get back the same amount. Instead, love your enemies and do good, and lend without any hope of return. You will have a great reward, and you will be sons of the Most High, for he himself is kind to the ungrateful and the wicked. (Luke 6:27–35)

Men and women work together. That is a given, engraved in all of human history and evident from the very first chapters of Scripture. Jesus says "Love one another; just as I have loved you," and nowhere does He say that the workplace is exempt from this command. For people who work for a living the implications of Jesus' words can be staggering. Living Christianity at work almost certainly requires you to carefully consider your attitudes and actions toward the other people on the job.

Exercise in Recognition #1: What If You Took Jesus at His Word?

The three Scripture passages presented above are all familiar to our culture. They are cited as often as any passage from Shakespeare. Many people would recognize them even if they had never been inside a church. And this familiarity has reduced their impact to that of clichés like "Safety First" or "Buy low and sell high."

Take a moment to look back over those passages. Reread the quotations presented on pages 51 and 52 and try to imagine what they would sound like if you had never heard them before. It might help to read them aloud.

While reading those passages, imagine what it would mean if you accepted Jesus at His word, if you really took His message to heart. Would next Monday be different if you went to work fully intending to live according to that commandment of love?

Take a few minutes to reread the passages and reflect before you read on.

William Law, a famous Anglican writer, once sadly noted that many Christians lead lives that fall far short of the mark. As he saw it, the problem was not that people try to lead lives of perfect love and fail, but that so many never really try at all. They just don't take the task seriously. His bluntness shows through his eighteenth-century English.

> Although the goodness of God and his rich mercies in Christ Jesus are sufficient assurance to us that he will be merciful to our unavoidable weaknesses, we have no reason to expect the same mercy toward those sins which we have not intended to avoid. . . . We cannot offer to God the service of angels. We cannot obey him as if we were in a state of perfection. But fallen men can do their best, and this is the perfection that is required of us.

Most men and women probably intend to be ethical, honest, and fair. Those are the basics—"For even sinners do that much" (Luke 6:33)—but Jesus asks more. To follow Him, we must go to work planning to love whoever is there and to treat them as we would wish to be treated. No one can succeed every time, but Christians need to try.

You are called upon to love your neighbors, even those neighbors who are unpleasant or who are your employers and competitors. It is essential to recognize that the people at work are exactly that—people. We have a powerful tendency to focus completely on immediate goals, on the job that must be done. We stop noticing other people and mentally transform them into elements of our own plan, into aids or obstacles, impediments or tools, until they are no longer seen as people at all.

The labels given people at work, their formal and informal "job titles," often suggest the pigeonholes to which they have been consigned. For example, most of us occasionally use descriptions that categorize people encountered at work as objects, instead of as individuals.

"My nine o'clock appointment"
"Those guys down at the warehouse"
"The receptionist"
"The rent-a-cop"
"The dingbat at Table 3"
"The next customer in line"
"The foreman from printing"
"The union steward"
"The P.R. lady from that publishing house"

Those titles are mostly innocuous. They name jobs people do and social roles they sometimes play. However, the automatic use of titles may reveal a perspective which prevents noticing that they are human—like us. If they aren't recognized as such then their needs are forgotten. If they can be mentally converted into office furniture or parts of the machinery, there is no perceived

51

need to love them or to even care about them. However, Jesus' command to love one another applies to these people as well.

Exercise in Recognition #2: Noticing the Real Person Behind the Job Title

Most people have a small group of friends at work who are clearly seen as real people. They all lunch together and even take in an occasional baseball game. They know the names of each other's children. But there is a second group of people on the job who are seen only occasionally outside of work, or only for formal business reasons. The chances are great that the real people in this group will be missed and relegated to job titles instead.

Try to remember someone you ran into at work over the last few days, someone you hardly know and relate to strictly for business purposes. What did you mentally call that person, other than his or her name? What job title did you confer on him or her?

This exercise stimulates the imagination. Its goal is to mentally flesh out the real person behind the job title. Fill in as many details as you can about the person you encountered. What do you know about the individual, beyond what he or she does at work? Since you probably don't have much information, let your imagination take over. Make up a background. Think of that person—"the patient in Dr. Stanfield's chair" or "the officer who brought in the summons"—away from work. Imagine that person in his or her living room watching TV or just petting the cat. Envision him or her in the kitchen or the garage, or on the telephone, getting a call from home. Fill in as many details as you can.

Now it's time to turn the tables. Try to imagine what it was like for that person to run into you at that recent meeting. How did you look to him or her? Try to step into this fantasy by imagining how that individual experienced the meeting with you.

Take several minutes for this exercise. It is challenging—but very useful.

Before you read on, pause and try to see the real person behind the job title.

A handy job title can mask the reality of the person, and working Christians have to strive steadily to break through this barrier. By mentally making others less than real people, you can feel free to use them as though they were tools. But if you recognize them as individuals, it will be less acceptable to you to treat them as equipment. You will begin to notice their needs, instead of yours alone.

Recognition of the real person is the first step in Christian love; it is a critical step toward appreciating others for themselves. It is a healing recognition because it opens your eyes. Your blindness is cured, your relationship restored to health. People do not love "the cleaning person" or really care about "the CPA who does the taxes." You only relate to "the tech in data control" for input and output. But you can love the real people behind those titles. Those moments of looking past function to humanity are truly graced by God.

Lumping individuals together into one big group is another mental trick used to ignore people. You cannot have a warm, personal relationship with "the steno pool" or "the sales staff." Grouping others together can lead to an evasion of any sense of responsibility or love for the individuals who comprise the group.

You automatically become more caring and compassionate when you recognize the individual person. The people who develop advertising for charities are aware of this fact. A sophisticated ad campaign would never focus on the headline, "One million children will starve in South America this year." That approach would leave the reader feeling powerless and overwhelmed by the immensity of the problem. Numbers have no warmth. No one can feed a million hungry children, so the reader would forget about them and turn the page.

Instead, a typical solicitation will show the face of a single hungry child and run a headline saying. "Carlos went to bed hungry again last night." The copy will supply his brother's name, and speak of the little cardboard house where he and his nine hungry brothers and sisters live. This approach prompts the reader to notice Carlos and recognize him in a way one cannot recognize "one million starving children." Carlos becomes a real person, and donors are willing to write a check for a real person in need.

Jesus looked at people as individuals and He loved them. Again and again He would recognize a single person in a group and minister directly to him or her alone. As He moved through a stifling crowd, a woman touching His cloak was cured—He turned to face her, saying "My daughter . . . your faith has restored you to health; go in peace." (Luke 8:43–48) Passing among the throngs in Jericho, He spotted the tax collector, Zacchaeus, sitting in a tree. "Zacchaeus, come down!" He called out, and in a few moments the wealthy sinner's life was transformed. (Luke 19:1–10) In that same city, blind Bartimaeus sat among a group of his fellows along the road and called out to Jesus. Jesus recognized him: "What do you want me to do for you?" Bartimaeus wanted sight, and it was granted. (Mark 10:45–52)

Jesus recognized human need in individual men and women. Almost all of the healing miracles were personal encounters between Jesus and one or two individuals who needed Him. Jesus demanded that His followers love and serve those around them by trying to meet their human wants. You can hide from that demand by staring at the faceless group and ignoring the people who make it up. But if you greet just one of those people as a real human being, the group will dissolve and the individuals will stand out in clear focus. In that moment, Jesus has the opportunity to grace the encounter with real healing—for both of you.

The habit of thinking of people in lumps is so ingrained that it can take a lot of work to break or even weaken it. This project may take several days, a week, or even longer. The exercise looks beyond the surface of the faceless group. By learning more about even a few individuals you will remember that all the rest are real people too.

Pick a group at work and find out a few things about some of the people within that group. You may have seen these individuals from time to time for years or may never have met even one of them face to face.

Take an index card and write the name of the group on the top. Keep it in your pocket or purse, or put it in a spot where you will see it at work. Now, find out the names of at least three of the people in that group and observe some bit of personal information about each of the three. Ted might hold his hip as though his back hurt. You may observe that Nancy likes cut flowers near her work station, and you might hear a Texas twang in David's voice. As you learn the names and notice the personal details, write them on your card. This will increase the amount of attention given to the uniqueness of each of the individuals within the group.

The exercise is complete when you have written down the names of three people and one or two personal details about each. By the time the task is finished, it will be harder for you to think of that group as a lump. You will be more conscious of the individuals as people.

Before you read on, find an index card and write the name of a group on it. Put it where you can see it the next time you go to work.

People who develop the habit of looking for those little human details will notice the real people within large groups more often. Jesus' example is clear—attend to the individual human beings in your world.

God is truly present in those other men and women. The hymn in Colossians 1 is a central Scripture, calling Jesus "The image of the unseen God and the first-born of all creation, for in him were created all things in heaven and on earth . . ." When Saul was knocked off his horse and blinded, Jesus said to him, "Saul, Saul, why are you persecuting me?" Saul, having no understanding of the question, asked who was speaking. The Lord responded: "I am Jesus and you are persecuting me." (Acts 9:4–6) Our Lord identified Himself with His followers. While some have taken this to mean that God is present only in the followers of Jesus, there is no excuse for limiting good will only to other Christians. All are creatures of God, brothers and sisters in God's family. To act otherwise would be to take on God's role in the judgment of human hearts.

If learning to love begins by recognizing people as individuals, it is completed by recognizing God in those people. In the absolutely astounding fact of the Incarnation, God forever entered the tattered reality of human life. Every person draws intrinsic worth from God's act of Creation, and that worth was affirmed in Jesus. Your task is to look for that spark of God in every man and woman you encounter, and respond to it with love.

Some people resist love and seem to go out of their way to earn rejection and dislike. It is hard to see God in these irritating people but important to do so. The crabby customer, the unfair supervisor, and the cheating accountant are all God's children. That they are bothersome does not mean you needn't work at loving them. Maybe they can even teach you something, if you let them.

Exercise in Recognition #4: Recognizing God in the Unattractive

Jesus said that He would return like a thief in the night. The disciples did not recognize Him on the road to Emmaus, although they knew Him well. There is no reason to believe that it would be easier for you to recognize Him if He were present before you.

It was widely believed in the Middle Ages that Jesus frequently took human form and traveled about the towns and countryside taking stock of the behavior of Christian men and women. Stories were often told of saints and sinners who met Jesus but did not recognize Him.

In these pious tales, Jesus almost always takes some unattractive form. He appears as a leper or beggar, and His behavior is often reported to be irritating or worse. Only after the other actors in the story have committed themselves, either by aiding the disguised Jesus or by rejecting Him, is His true identity revealed. The point of these stories, as simple-minded and superstitious as they may be, is that one never knows when or in what form Jesus might appear so that the best course of behavior is to treat everyone as if he or she might turn out to be the Savior in disguise.

Learn from your displeasure with certain people at work, from those who thwart or hamper the task at hand, or who irritate everyone around them. Use your feelings of irritation as a signal to remember the medieval stories. Whenever those feelings strike, take a moment to pretend that this nettlesome individual is actually Jesus in disguise, and that, like the disciples, your eyes have been closed to His presence. Perhaps you will then see some spark of God, or at least experience the other person through more open eyes.

Call to mind a recent troublesome encounter at work. Who else was involved? Can you recognize God's presence in that person? If that individual had been Jesus in disguise, what might He have learned about you from your actions?

Take a moment before you read on to reflect on God's presence in people who bother you.

Jesus had some definite ideas about how people are to relate to one another. He called on us to love and serve. Jesus is our Lord, yet He washed the disciples' feet.

"Do you understand," he said, "what I have done to you? You call me Master and Lord, and rightly; so I am. If I, then, the Lord and Master, have washed your feet, you should wash each other's feet. I have given you an example so that you may copy what I have done to you."

"I tell you most solemnly,
no servant is greater than his master,
no messenger is greater than the man who sent him."
(John 13:12–15)

You have an opportunity to see God when you recognize a fellow worker, customer, client, patient, or competitor as a real person. Jesus made it clear that He is present in all of us. "I tell you solemnly, in so far as you did this to one of the least of these brothers of mine, you did it to me." (Matthew 25:40)

6

Learning to Think Like a Christian: Component Four— Applying Reason and Learning from Experience

PEOPLE LEARN FROM EXPERIENCE. NOBODY CONTINues to wear shoes that hurt their feet if they can help it. If the boss yells at workers for coming in late, they leave their homes a bit earlier. A real estate agent who gains three listings in a single week by going door to door with calendars will have more printed and keep working the neighborhoods. It is human nature to notice and remember what works and what doesn't.

The progress made by applying reason to experience is impressive in the world of technology. Technological development, after all, is no more mysterious than people paying careful attention to how a job is done and coming up with better ways of doing it. The history of technology is a history of one improvement leading to another, of each innovation opening the way for one more.

Of course, between the invention of the wheel and the five-speed, turbo-charged BMW, there was a progression of revolutionary inventions and tiny improvements. Each of these steps, large or small, was accomplished because

59

someone paid close attention to how the work was getting done and learned from that experience.

Because of this steady improvement in our tools, we work better and faster than our ancestors ever could have imagined. One person working with a diesel skip loader can move more earth in a day than a hundred men armed with shovels and wheelbarrows could carry in a month. A single bookkeeper with a desk-top computer can generate more financial reports in a given amount of time than a dozen accountants could have only a generation ago.

In the arena of technology a great deal has been learned by applying reason to experience. In the realm of morality, such steady upward progress is harder to discern. There are those who pointedly deny that applying reason to experience has gotten us anywhere at all in the moral arena.

Two extreme positions exist today—and have in fact existed for centuries—within the church, and the debate continues in university departments of philosophy and theology. One extreme celebrates human reason, arguing that the moral truths that God gave man at the time of creation can be discovered through human reason and observation. This argument holds that common moral patterns are to be found in every human society, and that these patterns reflect God's natural laws. For example, murder and incest are universally condemned, and stealing is almost always prohibited. People recognize these principles of God's and learn about them by studying human societies.

The other extreme position holds that the whole process is hopeless. It contends that human reason has been so degraded by sin that it can yield nothing of moral value. The only valid source of moral direction is God's free grace, available through the word of Scripture and the direct, personal revelations of God's will to individuals. Human reason can only interfere with the workings of grace and lead to self-delusion, self-glorification, and more sin.

The great majority of current Christian ethical thinkers actually fall between these two extremes. They recognize both the validity and the inherent limits of human reason. These thinkers hold that moral reasoning reflects human striving to grow closer to God, that it is our response to His grace and His freely chosen action of lifting us up. The two need not be seen as working in opposition.

Reason is an important part of thinking like a Christian. It is not sufficient all by itself, though, as the human capacity for delusion and self-deception leave reason flawed and open to error. Pride in mankind's very real technological achievements can lead to a mistaken belief that we can answer all our own moral questions. Grace is also a critical component, and Christian moral decision making must draw upon the resources of Scripture and prayer, areas addressed in later chapters.

Even with its limits, reason is of value in moral life. Among the fruits of moral reasoning have been evolving codes of conduct, gradually clearer ideas about what is and is not right to do. These codes can be individual, endorsed by a particular group, or broadly shared by a society.

Individuals develop personal principles based on their particular experience. For example, a telephone equipment salesman may discover that if he explains the available options very quickly, it sounds as though they can be purchased only as a package. If he runs through the list and immediately asks for an order, the confused customer often stammers and orders all of the services instead of only one or two. The salesman may decide that his tactic is intentionally confusing and therefore not completely honest. The result might be a decision on his part to speak slowly and clearly during the critical twenty seconds of the sales pitch, even if this change cuts down the number of his orders. This is a personal principle developed through experience and reason. As people mature in their moral life, their principles become clearer and more refined.

Groups develop shared codes of ethics which gradually

evolve through the experience of living and doing business together. For example, most professional organizations have written ethical codes, and membership in the organization implies an acceptance of that code. In the thirteenth century, the silversmiths' guild had clear rules on who could and could not use the guild's distinctive stamp. In our time the attorney's Bar Association has strict rules on maintaining the privacy of client records. Military officers, civil engineers, independent truckers, teachers, doctors, and contractors all have codes of ethics developed by their professional and trade organizations.

Over time these develop and change. For example, in times past it might have been impossible for anyone but the son of a silversmith to join the guild; and until recent years women could not enter most unions, and racial discrimination was long both open and condoned. Such practices are now generally prohibited.

Finally, societies slowly develop shared moral norms. These broad social norms also gradually change over time, and some note a slow but perceptible movement toward a higher moral order. The centuries have seen major changes such as the worldwide abolition of slavery, the almost universal rejection of infanticide as population control, the gradual erosion of sexual and racial discrimination, and an increased sense of human interdependence and mutual responsibility. This spiraling upward movement is evidence that even on a social level mankind learns from experience and, painfully and ever so slowly, through the application of reason.

The fruits of experience and reason in ethical living are not mathematically precise answers to questions or prepackaged moral guidelines for the complex situations of life. Rather, reason is a part of the process of discovering appropriate responses to life's perplexing questions. Reason grounded in biblical faith and rooted in divine grace can help a Christian discover what action is called for in the present moment of life. The biblical word for knowledge always includes both theory and action. The finest fruits of reason and experience are not theoretically correct answers, but concrete loving actions.

There are as many ways to exercise moral reason as there are ways to pray. And just as one learns to make prayer a part of life, one can learn to use reason more consciously when making work-related ethical decisions. Two approaches will be shared here. The first develops a careful respect for the pooled ethical judgments of your fellow workers. The second introduces a tool for becoming a more effective observer of your own moral life.

Formal codes of ethics are a common part of business and professional life. It is quite likely that you are a member of a group with such a list of dos and don'ts for conducting business. Some are only a page or two long, and others fill books with principles and subprinciples, discussions, explanations, and detailed examples.

Exercise in Reason #1: Codes of Ethics

Whether you are an auto retailer, a social worker, an independent trucker, a loan officer, a claims adjuster, a direct mail order business woman, or an Episcopal priest, it is almost certain that some professional or business organization has taken the time to think through and write down a code of ethics for your line of work. When it comes to such codes, people fall into four groups:

- Group 1 is quite sure that there is no written code of ethics for their group.
- Group 2 simply doesn't know whether or not there is an applicable code of ethics.
- Group 3 knows (or strongly suspects) there is a code of ethics, but doesn't know what it is.
- Group 4 knows there is a code of ethics, and knows something about what it has to say.

What group are you in? Carefully review the list, and decide which is most like you.

As a test, think about your most recent day at work.

63

Now, try to remember something you did that was *covered* by an ethical code. What was this action, and what do you recall the code saying about it? Now, look back at the list of groups. Did you change your mind about where you belong?

Before you read on, test your recall of your profession or trade's code of ethics.

"What's the point?" you may well ask. "Shouldn't Christians study the Bible instead of human codes of ethics?" The problem phrase in that sentence is "instead of." Replace it with "and also" and the statement makes perfect sense. Working Christians should study the Bible *and also* the ethical norms of their business or profession.

Written ethical codes are the result of refined reason. No individual can have all of the experiences of a large group of men and women working in the same field. Codes are developed when serious-minded people sit down together and review their experience of what makes for ethical and honest practice in their particular kind of work. They search for the best answers to such questions as, "How should we behave so that we can trust each other, and our customers can trust us? What should we and our customers be able to expect of each other?"

Usually years of study and a good deal of heated argument go into writing such codes. Those who prepared the ethical standards for your line of work have given more time to thinking about the problems than you have. There is no virtue whatsoever in dismissing their work and repeating the process yourself, as though the questions had never been considered before.

Think back to the four groups. If you found yourself in Group 1, certain that there is no written code of ethics for your business group, or in Group 2, not knowing whether or not there is a code, start looking. Such a code probably exists. A good way to find out about it is by contacting your local business or professional organization, or your local union. (Even if you aren't a member, you can get the information!) If they can't help you, they will know whom to call. What you don't know *will* hurt you. How can you ever hope to rise to the higher levels if you don't know what is expected of you?

If you fall into either Group 3 or 4 then you know something about the code for your line of work, although it may not be much. Look for a copy of the code, get it, and reread it. Even if you think you know it pretty well, this is a good time for a review. Studying that code can be an important part in the upward evolution of your own moral standards.

This chapter began with the statement that people learn from experience. Careful observers will notice some predictable cause-and-effect relationships between their actions and what happens afterwards. All of us recognize some immediate relationships: turn the key and the car starts; buy a bigger sign and attract more customers.

But there are some consequences that take longer to show up, and you might not notice those as readily. For example, a plastics dealer may hope to be of help by sharing some personal leads with the new sales rep in the office. Some weeks later she may learn that this generosity made the new worker anxious and uncomfortable, that it was interpreted as a sign of low confidence in his ability to generate business. The "helpful" act backfired.

No one would reasonably fault the dealer for sharing the leads or hold her directly responsible for the new co-worker's problems. How could she have predicted the outcome? However, if she doesn't learn from experience, if she fails to recognize the relationship between her helpfulness and this co-worker's anxiety, she may continue to do things that hamper his work performance. In the moral arena, the consequences of greatest importance are often not immediately apparent.

It is harder to recognize relationships when the consequences take a long time to become evident. A notebook is a marvelous tool for recognizing such relationships. Many people imagine scientists as people with microscopes, computers and exotic glass and electronic devices. Scientists actually do use such instruments, but every scientist in the world also has at least one notebook, and the best of them recognize that careful record keeping is their most valuable asset.

Records are important because human memory is so faulty. Actually, memory is adequate for storage, but retrieval of stored information is sometimes spotty. Who hasn't agreed to bring some needed paperwork to a meeting, only to remember the promise ten minutes after the meeting has begun? The information about the commitment was stored, it just wasn't pulled out at the right time. A brief note on a to-do list might have prevented that embarrassment.

Another problem with memory is the tendency to recall the most recent occurrence or the most vivid event. For example, a hardware dealer may have sold equipment to Mr. Stomer dozens of times. Mr. Stomer has been a good customer, and he has always met his obligations. Then one day he bounces a check—once, when the hardware dealer really needs the cash to cover an order for the store. The dealer's discomfort may be enough to ensure that he never quite trusts Stomer again, even if he doesn't bounce another check.

The only way to get past the problems of memory is to write things down. Scientists make observations and then write down what they notice. Later they can go back over their notes, sort through their impressions, and reach conclusions. In reviewing their records, relationships become apparent which weren't obvious earlier. Changes can be seen which might have taken weeks or months to develop. Good scientists learn from experience more efficiently than the rest of us, because they are often more careful observers, and they keep good records.

If the hardware dealer carefully checked his business records, assuming that his transactions with Mr. Stomer were noted, he would find a pattern of consistent honesty. He would probably recognize the bounced check as an oversight, and trust him in the future.

An excellent way to learn about your own ethical decision making is to keep a notebook on the choices you make. Of course, you won't record them all—there are too many for complete record keeping. But you might obtain valuable insight by recording one each day. Keeping brief notes and going over them from time to time can be important steps in observing your own moral life, and they can be especially helpful in learning about those moral decisions whose consequences are not immediately evident.

The first step is to get a notebook and pick a time to write in it. Setting up a regular habit of record keeping is the key to the success of the entire process. Think about when you could *really* spend five minutes or so every day to record your ethical decisions. Try to do it at the same time every day.

Each time you work with your notebook, write down *one* decision you made in the previous twenty-four hours. Write about a decision that seemed to have ethical implications.

Begin by writing the date and a brief description of the decision that identifies the central issue.

June 8

We got a new order from Jackson today. He wants us to extend him credit beyond the usual 30 days. He says his working cash is tight, and if he can't get the parts from us, he'll have to lay off three men. He was quite clear that he could pay me in 60 days. I don't like extending the credit policy—pretty soon every short-on-cash contractor will be at my order desk.

Next, write about the action you took, and how you chose it.

I decided not to give him the credit. I took a few minutes, and even prayed over it. I realized that I've got some employees of my own, and they deserve a boss who keeps the business sound. But I also decided to call my banker and encourage him to give Jackson a loan—he's been a good credit risk in the past.

Finally, write down a date when you can evaluate this decision and see how things worked out. If you will need to do something special, such as making a phone call or checking the papers, write that down along with the date. Then, when the time comes, think about the ways your action helped or hurt others, or reflected your caring, and write that down.

August 30
I called Jackson this afternoon. He's out of the contracting business. He tried to get the loan, but his income hadn't been steady enough to carry it off. He said his men all went to work with a bigger firm across town and he's working as a foreman for them, too. I think this worked out well. He apparently wasn't much of a businessman. He may do better this way.

In addition to such planned reviews it is helpful to sit from time to time and read through your notes for a while. You may find all sorts of useful information in them, and notice some relationships which were not evident as the events were taking place.

Exercise in Reason #2: Writing the First Page in Your Notebook

Take the time *now* to write a few notes about an ethical decision made at work in the last few days. It is important to take this step before you go on. Concrete action is likely to insure the transition of what sounds like a good idea into a workable reality. Of course, you won't be able to do the followup now, but try picking a date when it would be possible to learn how things turned out. And, before you forget about it, pick up a spiral notebook. It may be the best tool for learning you ever use.

Before you read on, practice writing about an ethical decision.

People learn by applying reason to experience. Americans are a practical people who tend to view life as a series of problems just waiting to be solved. The application of reason to experience, both your own reason and that shared by the others in your field, may indeed help you solve the most important problem of all—how best to respond to the presence of God in your life.

7

Learning to Think Like a Christian: Component Five— Looking for Direction in Scripture

CHRISTIANS PROFESS A REMARKABLE BELIEF CONcerning the Bible. Since the earliest years of the Church, Scripture has been known as the word of God, as the central message from Him to humanity for all time and all places revealed and guaranteed as true by the working of the Holy Spirit. This is a very unusual perspective. But then, Christians are supposed to be unusual people. Paul summarized the importance of Scripture in his second letter to Timothy.

> You must keep to what you have been taught and know to be true; remember who your teachers were, and how, ever since you were a child, you have known the holy scriptures—from these you can learn the wisdom that leads to salvation through faith in Christ Jesus. All Scripture is inspired by God and can profitably be used for teaching, for refuting error, for guiding people's lives and teaching them to be holy. This is how the man who is dedicated to

God becomes fully equipped and ready for any good work. (2 Timothy 3:14-17)

Just how is that to happen? How can a very long book, written over the course of ten centuries by dozens of individual authors, teach Christians to be holy? Moreover, how can it be applied to the world of work?

These questions have been answered in many ways over the centuries of Christian history since the Council of Hippo drew up the first canon of inspired books. In this brief chapter we cannot even touch on the deep and rich history of biblical research, scholarship, and theology. We will present a view of Scripture to be used for moral guidance, but we must assert that it is only one way among many. It contains the strengths and weaknesses common to any single viewpoint on so complex a topic as the Bible.

The Scriptures deal with a social world which is different from ours in some ways, but very much like it in other ways. We may wonder how the writings of a group of precapitalist, preindustrial people could possibly pertain to the complexities of modern economic life. Modern historical research has demonstrated, however, that Jesus and His contemporaries were economically quite sophisticated. It is clear that they understood many of our basic economic principles.

The people of that time used money, made loans, and charged interest. Property was bought and sold at a profit. Beyond that, the people of Judea and Galilee were part of a complex international commercial trade network extending throughout the known world. The ancient Phoenicians, and later the Greeks and Romans, built up a remarkable economic system which worked very well, even by our contemporary standards. Jesus' contemporaries kept books, maintained accounts, and managed exchange rates. Our own economic crimes—fraud, overcharging, and deceitful contracting—were all well documented in the four Gospels.

Jesus' own economic sophistication is shown in His

71

teachings. In the Parable of the Talents (Matthew 25: 14–30) He tells the story of a wealthy man who leaves his employees to manage his fortune while he is traveling. Each of the three servants is entrusted with a large sum of money. Two of them go into business with their funds and succeed in doubling their master's money before his return home. He is understandably pleased with the profit and promises them greater responsibility and reward in the future. The third servant, fearful, buries his share of the master's money in the ground and returns it without increase. The master, enraged at this failure to manage his property profitably, says: "Well then, you should have deposited my money with the bankers, and on my return I would have recovered my capital with interest."

This is not a story told by a financial illiterate. Had Jesus been speaking to a world without connection to ours, our present faith might seem irrelevant and even impossible. But such is not the case. Jesus understood the concepts of profit, investments, banking, and interest. The modern reader can grasp the meaning of this parable because we share the same understanding of investment, money-lending, and financial responsibility. Indeed, this story could be fully updated without changing anything but the titles of the major characters.

A millionaire was going to travel abroad for a year, and divided his capital among his three portfolio managers. . . .

Even if you accept the fact that the Scriptures really do have an impact on your work life, the initial question still remains. How can the Bible be used for refuting error, for guiding people's lives, and teaching them to be holy? More exactly, how can the teachings in the Bible be applied to what you do on Monday morning?

The gospel is not a point-by-point rule book, like the Securities and Exchange Commission code on the management of investments, nor was it meant to be. To look for specific and concrete direction in the New Testament is dangerous in two ways. First, it leads right back to the obsession with rules and proper management of minutiae that plagued the Scribes and Pharisees. Remember, they already had a rule book, the Law, and it had not brought them salvation. In Paul's phrase, the law was the "tutor" which prepared them to receive Jesus, but the law was not the final message.

> The Law was to be our guardian until the Christ came and we could be justified by faith. Now that that time has come we are no longer under that guardian, and you are, all of you, sons of God through faith in Christ Jesus. (Galatians 3:24–26)

The other risk of looking for specific and concrete direction in the New Testament is that such a search can overshadow the main point of Jesus' message. If you read the Parable of the Talents to mean "You are morally responsible to earn the highest possible return on your employer's money" you will miss the point altogether. Jesus is not teaching about acceptable rates of return—He is talking about the call to responsible discipleship.

That is the cornerstone of the New Testament. The Christian moral response is derived from faith in a person, Jesus, rather than from faith in a set of concepts or laws. Discipleship is not a moral abstraction. It is an entire way of life based on the historical flesh-and-blood example of Jesus. The call to discipleship and our response to it are the muscle and sinew of Christian moral life. As His disciple, your choice is not to follow a specific set of rules, a given ethical code. Rather, it is to follow a specific Savior.

Exercise in Reading #1: The Vine

The Gospel is clear. We are invited to respond to God's love by becoming followers of Jesus Christ. Jesus, the physical embodiment of God's love, does not call us to be spectators, or even imitators, but rather to be participants in His Kingdom. Consider the following selection from the Gospel of John.

> I am the true vine,
> and my father is the vinedresser.
> Every branch in me that bears no fruit
> he cuts away,
> and every branch that does bear fruit he prunes
> to make it bear even more.
> You are pruned already,
> by means of the word that I have spoken to you.
> Make your home in me, as I make mine in you.
> As a branch cannot bear fruit all by itself,
> but must remain part of the vine,
> neither can you unless you remain in me.
> I am the vine,
> you are the branches.
> Whoever remains in me, with me in him,
> bears fruit in plenty;
> for cut off from me you do nothing. (John 15:1–5)

Jesus does not say, "Follow this list of rules." He says, "Make your home in me, as I make mine in you." Take a moment to reflect on the difference between these two statements.

Spend a few minutes reflecting on your relationship to the vine before you read on.

The basic question remains. How does the Scripture guide us to be holy? How does it prepare us for good works, strengthening the bond between vine and branches? How does Scripture form the disciple? The full answer depends, of course, on the grace of God. However there are some human insights which may make the process clearer.

The Bible is a collection of stories which were told and retold by the people to whom God revealed Himself. The people of Israel knew that God had spoken to Abraham and the patriarchs, that He had led them out of slavery in Egypt and had remained with them. The Israelites loved to repeat the stories of their deliverance and God's action in their history because these stories gave them an identity.

Jesus was born a Jew, and therefore He inherited that rich tradition of stories. He also told stories, performed deeds witnessed by His followers, and taught lessons which they remembered. Finally, He died on the cross and rose again from the dead. His early followers told and retold the stories of His life and teachings. They repeated the stories which He had told. They set those stories down, both in writing and in the framework of liturgy and worship. Those stories defined who they were and give us our own identities as well.

Exercise in Reading #2: Remembering Family Stories

Almost every family has stories it repeats over and over again. Gerald Matlock, the grandfather of one of the authors, was a famous storyteller in Kendall County, Illinois. Scout troops often came to his home to hear stories of the days before the roads, when Indians and pioneers slipped past each other in the dark woods. He told stories of gypsies and horse thieves and how his own grandfather operated a way station on the underground railroad to freedom. Listening to him, they came to know their history five generations deep. They learned who they were.

Children light up when their parents talk about the days, way back in time (maybe even ten years ago), when they were babies. Hearing your mother or father talk about your own infancy is exciting—it tells you who you are. Little children urge repeatedly, "Tell about the time. . . ."

Perhaps you can remember one of the stories repeated about your childhood. Or can you recall an often-told family story about someone else or some other time in your family history?

Think about that story. What does it say about your family? What might it say about who *you* are?

Reflect on a family story before you read on.

The Gospel stories are similar to family stories. They are the stories of the one you follow, and the stories of who you are to become. Just as your family's stories shaped your opinion of yourself as a child, the biblical tales form your portrait of yourself as a Christian adult. The more deeply they penetrate your memory, the more fully they will shape your sense of self. In this way the gospel forms disciples. As the Bible—the shared memory of 2,000 years of Christian men and women—becomes your personal memory as well, the knowledge of who you really are will grow—a child of God and a follower of the truest teacher, Jesus.

That process was already begun, years ago, when you first heard the story of Jesus. For longtime church members and fairweather friends alike, there are Bible stories so familiar, stories heard so often they are a part of your memory, that it is as if they are stories about yourself or your family.

Exercise in Reading #3: Familiar Stories

The following lines are the first sentences of a number of very familiar passages from the life of Jesus. Try to recognize them. You may even find that you know them so well that their endings occur to you.

Now at this time Caesar Augustus issued a decree for a census of the whole world to be taken. (Luke 2:1)

After they had left, the angel of the Lord appeared to Joseph in a dream and said. ''Get up, take the child and his mother with you, and escape into Egypt and stay there until I tell you, because Herod intends

76

to search for the child and do away with him."
(Matthew 2:13)

By now it was getting very late, and his disciples
came up to him and said, "This is a lonely place
and it is getting very late, so send them away and
they can go to the farms and villages round about,
to buy themselves something to eat." (Mark 6:36)

Six days later, Jesus took with him Peter and
James and his brother John and led them up a high
mountain where they could be alone. (Matthew 17:1)

But the man was anxious to justify himself and
said to Jesus, "And who is my neighbour?" Jesus
replied, "A man was once on his way down from
Jerusalem to Jericho and fell into the hands of brig-
ands. . . ." (Luke 10:29–30)

The next day the crowds who had come up for the
festival heard that Jesus was on his way to Jerusalem. They took branches of palm and went out to
meet him, shouting, "Hosanna! Blessings on the
King of Israel, who comes in the name of the Lord."
(John 12:12–13)

On the first day of the week, at the first sign of
dawn, they went to the tomb with the spices they
had prepared. (Luke 24:1)

How many are familiar? Seven stories were begun using nine sentences in all. It is quite possible that a person
who considered himself only marginally conversant with
the Scriptures would recognize four or five and would
remember, in a general way, the rest of the stories. The
remarkable thing is that these stories span the life and
review the major teachings of Jesus. Are you surprised
by how much of the Gospel is already known to you?
If you did not recognize any of the stories from these

glimpses, it would be well for you to look them up. They may turn out to be very familiar, even if you didn't know them right away.

Reflect a moment on how much Scripture is already familiar to you before you read on.

For Scripture to do its proper work, that of making you a disciple, it must become a part of your own memory. While there is much comfort to be had in quoting recognizable passages line by line, this is not the sort of memory we suggest that you cultivate. Rather, we mean a familiarity with the events and the stories that comprise our Christian heritage. Scripture is not merely a record of the long-ago Hebrew and early Christian communities. It is a means to encounter the living God who continues to act in your life. As a member of the believing community, you continue to live out the story of Jesus.

This is not a one-step process of memorization or subjective recall. The experience of Scripture is more than an internal mental exercise. The living God continues to be intrusive, using your memory, imagination, reason and will, challenging you to respond to His initiative. The biblical story and your personal story intersect, and at that point of meeting, God calls you to deeper discipleship.

Jesus compared the word of God to seed falling in the human heart. In some hearts it grows and in others it withers or is choked off.

> And the one who received the seed in rich soil is the man who hears the word and understands it; he is the one who yields a harvest and produces now a hundredfold, now sixty, now thirty. (Matthew 13:23)

Nature produces nourishing grain—even the cleverest botanist cannot produce a single grain of wheat by his own actions. However, the seeds can be planted, watered, and fertilized by us and the weeds can be pulled before they crowd out the harvest.

You contribute to God's action in your own life by studying the Bible. In this way you cooperate with grace. The following exercises are intended to help you participate more fully in the shared memory which is Scripture.

The first exercise is over five hundred years old. Traditionally called meditation, it uses the imagination to add sparkle and life to the experience of the written word. As we noted earlier, many of the stories about Jesus are so well known that it can be hard to see further than the story itself. It is tempting to say, "Oh, yeah, the Prodigal Son. I know that one." At that point the eyes may keep reading, but the mind shuts off. Little new information gets filtered into memory.

This exercise can be used for any of the narrative portions of Scripture, and is especially appropriate for the Gospels. They are lively stories, full of warmth and humanity. They are also crucial stories for those who would become more Christ-like at work or anywhere else. The exercise takes from twenty to thirty minutes, but they are minutes well spent. The story chosen for this example is the calling of the first disciples, taken from the Gospel of St. Mark.

Exercise in Reading #4: Meditation on the Scriptures

Read the passage, preferably aloud. Adults rarely read aloud to themselves, yet the sounds of the words add to their impact. Read through the entire story, rather than just a verse or two. While the example below is kept brief for illustration, the Bible is best understood in context. A longer passage is more likely to contain clues about the happenings of the time. For example, the parable of the good Samaritan is placed, not coincidentally, in the chapter of Luke immediately following an incident in which Jesus is quite callously denied hospitality in a Samaritan village. The parable itself, one of the greatest

79

passages in the Gospels, draws even more meaning from its placement in the larger context of Luke's Gospel.

Use your imagination as you read the passage and add details of your own. What does the story's setting look like? How is the weather? How do the characters look? Try to mentally add detail while reading the passage aloud, slowly and reflectively.

> As he was walking along by the Sea of Galilee he saw Simon and his brother Andrew casting a net in the lake—for they were fishermen. And Jesus said to them, "Follow me and I will make you fishers of men." And at once they left their nets and followed him.
>
> Going on a little further, he saw James son of Zebedee and his brother John; they too were in their boat, mending their nets. He called them at once and, leaving their father Zebedee in the boat with the men he employed, they went after him. (Mark 1:16–20)

Step One: Enter the Life of One of the Characters

Now that you have read the story, you will role-play the events as they occur. First, "become" Simon in your mind—do this in the same way as a child might play "let's pretend." What is the fishing like on the side of the lake? Imagine the sound of the small waves slapping against the boat, or the feel of the wet nets in your hand. What is it about the man on the bank that attracts you? How do you feel about leaving your livelihood? Imagine what you might do with the boat, or with the fish already caught. Do you intend to return later that afternoon or tomorrow? Give yourself a few minutes to think about what it might be like to be Simon, long before he ever imagined that he would become "Peter."

Step Two: Mentally Enter the Life of Another
of the Characters

Now choose another character. Zebedee might be a good
one. Imagine watching your own sons walk away with a
stranger, leaving you with the hired hands! How would
you feel if your child followed some vagabond teacher?
Might you not be angry, or horrified? Or perhaps Zebedee approved of his sons' decision and even encouraged
them to go. The Scriptures do not say. Give yourself a
few minutes to get in touch with how it might have been.

Continue in this way for as long as you like. Take on
any of the characters, even Jesus. One of the authors has
an imaginary person he often places in the scene, a "re-
luctant disciple," who usually scratches his head and
wonders "What's going on here?" Take as much time as
you need at this point before continuing the exercise.

Step Three: Apply the Story to Your Own Life

Imagination has now made the story more vivid, in a way
that hearing it read from the pulpit could never do. It has
already become a part of your own personal memory. It
is time to stop the mental role-playing and look at the
story's meaning in your real life.

Try to sort out the different scenes of the story and
how they apply to your situation. Are you busy with your
employment, with keeping yourself and your family fed?
How do you experience the Lord's call? As an exciting
invitation or as a threat to your usual way of doing things?
Are there times when you would leave your nets behind
and follow Him? Are there other times when you would
stay in the boat, doing what you know well? It may be
comforting to remember that after the crucifixion, Simon
and the others returned to their fishing—what they knew
best—and they had to be called to shore by the risen Lord
all over again. Certainly in all of our lives there are times
when we respond and times when we choose the solace
of the familiar, the safe.

The exercise is relatively simple, and it can also be fun. It activates religious imagination and so causes the biblical stories to become more deeply seated in your memory. There is still another step you must take as a working Christian: you must bring the Scriptures into direct contact with your job.

The next exercise is designed to do exactly that. It places your memory of the story of Jesus face to face with your experience of the working world. Again, it can be done with any portion of the Bible, but the exercise seems most appropriate with the parables. Those teaching stories were related by Jesus with the direct intention of making His listeners look at things differently. (For your convenience a full listing of the parables is provided in the appendix of this book.) The parables also frequently deal at least on the surface with the matter-of-fact issues of economic life. What better tools could there be for opening your eyes to the influence of Scripture on the choices you make at work?

*Exercise in Reading #5: Bringing the Bible Along
to Work*

This exercise contains two steps. First, read through a passage of Scripture, in this case one of the parables, slowly and carefully. Close your Bible and review the passage in your mind. Try to remember as many details of the story as you can. Reopen the Bible and reread the passage to be sure you have remembered it correctly. Sometimes your recollection will be inaccurate. If this happens you will need a reminder.

As an example, read this passage from the Gospel of Matthew.

> What sort of servant, then, is faithful and wise enough for the master to place him over his household to give them their food at the proper time? Happy that servant if his master's arrival finds him at this employment. I tell you solemnly, he will place

him over everything he owns. But as for the dishonest servant who says to himself, "My master is taking his time" and sets about beating his fellow servants and eating and drinking with drunkards, his master will come on a day he does not expect and will cut him off and send him to the same fate as the hypocrites, where there will be weeping and grinding of teeth. (Matthew 24: 45–51)

Now close the book, review it in your mind, and then check your memory. Try to be sure that you have it right.

The second step is to recall the passage at work. If you read it in the morning before work, you will be able to bring it to mind several times during the day. Mentally review the story and see if there is any connection between the parable and your experience right then and there at work.

For now, remember your most recent day at work. Can you recall a time when you had a few moments for reflection? Now see if there is some point of contact between your job and the parable of the responsible servant?

What resources has God entrusted to you? Are there people who look to you for guidance or care? How are you discharging your responsibilities to them and to God? Reflect on this for a minute or so.

Take a minute to look for connections between your life and the parable from Matthew before reading on.

These exercises will be most helpful to you if you do them many times over a period of months or even years. Scripture does not enter your mind or pervade your life automatically. The conversion of the heart is not a "one time thing" that never needs to be repeated. It is a process, much more like a journey than a destination. Scripture is quite clear on the point that faith makes an impact on action—any faith which does less falls short of the biblical ideal.

Meditating on the Bible stories and bringing them to work with you will inevitably cause some tension. When it seems more comfortable to stay in the boat, Jesus' call will feel like an imposition. This is as it should be. Our Lord's message is not to be comfortable with the way things are, to be successful by the standards of the marketplace. If this were His desire, He would have told Simon where the fish were and left him alone and slightly better off because of the day's good catch.

That tension is caused by the encounter with God. The Scriptures are challenges. They can make you nervous by highlighting the gaps between what you are and what you are called to be, between what you do now and what you could do if you really chose to follow Jesus. Resolve that conflict by drawing closer to the path of our Risen Lord and the purpose of the Scriptures will indeed be fulfilled in you. Scripture is for teaching, for refuting error, for guiding people's lives and leading them to be holy.

As the Bible stories become your stories as well, as they sink deeper and deeper into your personal memory, they become your lens for viewing the world. Deep memory lies below the surface of consciousness, shaping all experience, imparting a new meaning to life. At this point Scripture becomes the context of your own personal story, and the God who reveals Himself in Scripture begins to reveal Himself to you in new and surprising ways.

8

Learning to Think Like a Christian: Component Six— Seeking Guidance from the Church

And to some, his gift was that they should be apostles; to some, prophets; to some, evangelists; to some, pastors and teachers; so that the saints together make a unity in the work of service, building up the body of Christ. In this way we are all to come to unity in our faith and in our knowledge of the Son of God, until we become the perfect Man, fully mature with the fullness of Christ himself. . . . If we live by the truth and in love, we shall grow in all ways into Christ, who is the head by whom the whole body is fitted and joined together, every joint adding its own strength, for each separate part to work according to its function. So the body grows until it has built itself up, in love. (Ephesians 4:11–16)

No one was meant to live the Christian life alone. Paul did not chronicle a church consisting of holy loners, but always of men and women in groups welded together by God's love. No one can do it alone because there are too many jobs to be done, too many challenges to be met, and too many ways to get lost and confused. Until we reach perfection—whenever that might be—Jesus gives us the gift of each other. He promised that where two or three met in His name, His presence would join their individual gifts together. As Paul wrote, "every joint adding its own strength, for each separate part to work according to its function."

The church is more than a building with a steeple. The church can be seen and experienced in different ways, but at its most universal level, the church is made up of all those men and women who are trying to follow Jesus in their lives. If you would be His follower, the surest way to travel is in the company of other believers.

You need the church—other believers—in your working life, because it is unlikely that you will find yourself surrounded by people who take the Gospel seriously at your job. Paul could not have imagined a society as thoroughly secular as ours. He lived in a world where people debated in earnest if it was permissible to pick a few handfuls of grain for lunch on the Sabbath or necessary to pay tithes on mint from the garden. These issues can appear trivial to us, the neurotic fixations of a small-minded people, but these discussions reflected the real concerns of a people who wanted to live according to the will of God. They saw no line separating religious from economic life. In today's workplace, it is considered impolite or ridiculous to even mention religion.

Most people, including many devout believers, rarely discuss the religious dimensions of decisions made on the job. How would you explain to Paul that it is possible for people to take jobs, work for years, even run giant industries and lead governments, without once discussing religion? The idea would make him dizzy. But most of us work in a world where religion is a stranger and religious people a curiosity. You need other believers—the church—to remind you that religious questions are the most important questions to ask.

If religion isn't commonly discussed, the sensitive person won't bring it up in situations where others might consider it an impolite subject. Religious people need to talk about religious issues, though, to test their thinking and to draw support from others. They need to find settings where that is encouraged, where they won't be stared at for bringing up an idea like the Christian's call to serve the poor. Those settings can best be found within the church.

There are a number of possible points of contact with other people in the church. For the individual believer, church men and women appear to be divided into three groups. The first of these is made up of the active members of the denominational body, those who directly participate in denominational organizations larger than the local congregation. They are both lay people and clergy. For example, a bishop is by definition an active member of the denominational body, while a lay woman elected to a diocesan finance board would also be a member. Denominational bodies range from the highly developed hierarchy of the Roman Catholic church, to the less structured, less centrally governed associations of individual congregations, such as the District Associations of the Baptists.

The second group is the local clergy. These men and women are often the major source of ethical and spiritual direction for the members of their congregations. When asked with whom they might discuss an important religious issue, many members would quickly respond, "With the pastor, of course."

The third group is the laity, those who may not be active in the denominational body but who are trying nonetheless to follow Jesus in their lives. This third group is in many ways the most important resource for the working Christian.

The church provides support and guidance at each level. Each group gives that support and guidance in its own way and with certain strengths and weaknesses. You can derive the most benefit from the church by making contact with members of each group.

The denominational body is what most people mean

when they refer to "organized religion." Most, although not all, congregations are affiliated with a larger denomination, whether Catholic or Swedenborgian, Southern Baptist, Missouri Synod Lutheran, or Congregationalist.

The denominational body has a long and honorable history. In New Testament times the apostles and elders in the church of Jerusalem made decisions about faith and morals. Paul and Timothy traveled from one town to another and "passed on the decisions reached by the apostles and elders in Jerusalem, with instructions to respect them." (Acts 16:4) Theirs may have been the first act of any church organization larger than a single congregation.

In the modern world the denominational body is composed of theologians, scholars, and church bureaucrats. These groups publish codes of belief and broad policy statements, develop international missionary boards, manage seminaries and send out denominational newsletters. They decide who may be ordained and who is or is not married in the eyes of the church. They authorize hymnals, select prayer books, and prepare rites of worship. They embody the organized expression of what makes the denomination special and unique.

For a number of reasons, the individual working Christian may have trouble seeing the relevance of this group's thoughts to working life. Those in the governing bodies of most denominations focus their attention on the demanding tasks of managing their denomination's affairs. Their teaching activity usually addresses either doctrinal issues within the denomination—"Shall we ordain women?"—or broad social concerns—"What should be the government's role in creating jobs for the poor?" Mundane issues such as, "Just how can one be a Christian and still sell appliances?" are rarely addressed at this level.

The majority of active Christian men and women never have the chance to sit and discuss their job problems with any members of this group. The denominational body usually carries out its teaching role through written statements. Whether addressing issues of ethics, economics, or worship, the body must write for everyone in the denomination. It is impossible to be specific and detailed when addressing so many different people. Therefore, church statements are usually written in general terms. Unfortunately, the individual Christian reading these statements may feel that they are too general to provide concrete answers to his or her questions. Denominational statements on work often sound like this:

> The culture which our age awaits will be marked by the full recognition of the dignity of human work, which appears in all its nobility and fruitfulness in the light of the mysteries of creation and redemption. Recognized as a form of the person, work becomes a source of creative meaning and effort.

This statement is part of a recent brilliantly argued instruction on Christian freedom, work, and liberation. In issuing such a statement, the denominational body is attempting to clarify the implications of the Gospel on daily life. But the need to make statements which apply to all can force the writers to use a language and style foreign to many potential readers.

When people are uncomfortable with this variety of prose they have a difficult time connecting the general theological or ethical statements with the facts of their daily lives. Nonetheless, some very important communication takes place when church members read these writings, and these statements do merit attention. Like the ethical codes discussed in an earlier chapter, doctrinal positions and other statements drafted by the churches represent the best current thought. When you read those statements, you compare your own thinking with that of the best minds in the denomination. The denominational body is often the bearer of profound religious truth, and you do well to draw upon that resource.

Catholic tradition places special emphasis on the writings of church leaders, the Pope and the bishops. The faithful Catholic has an obligation known as *obsequium religiosum*, variously translated as "submission," "due respect" or "obedience." The pastoral teachings of the church are seen as binding on the individual's moral life.

The religious press is a valuable tool in applying broad church statements to your daily life. Church newspapers and publications often carry both the general position papers and interpretive articles, which explain what the doctrine and statements of the denominational body mean to the individual. To keep in touch, read a church newspaper, magazine, or newsletter on a regular basis. Regular exposure to the thinking of the members of the body, even if limited to a few minutes a month, can be an important part of one's moral education.

As a member of a denomination you may already receive at least one religious newspaper or magazine. Do you read it? Survey data sadly indicates that the majority of church members do not. If you are one of those who have never developed a taste for religious periodicals, now might be a good time to try again. Set that church publication with the books and magazines you read. And then plan on a regular time to read it.

If you don't receive even a single church newspaper or magazine, consider subscribing to one. Ask your pastor or a friend to recommend a publication that he or she reads and finds useful. There are several hundred specifically Christian newspapers and magazines published in the United States alone. And, like any other type of publication, there are Christian magazines with different styles and philosophies. A selection is almost certainly available to you in your church library or local Christian bookstore, and those publications of broadest interest are often carried in the public libraries. By looking at several, you will find one that fits your interests as well as one that you will benefit from reading.

The church's second group is the local clergy. The local priest or minister is the most visible, and often the most available, representative of the church in the ordinary person's life. Talking with the pastor makes sense.

Many clergy women and men view counseling and guidance as an important part of their ministry, and they seek out opportunities to help. When you are having trouble figuring out what following Jesus means in your life, the local clergy provides a potential source of guidance.

It is the task of the clergy to give advice and encouragement to their congregations. The most common format is the sermon. The homily is an important part of most public worship services. The preacher's background and education provide expertise on Scripture and the teachings of the church. A good preacher is often a translator, taking those sources of knowledge and information and putting them into understandable terms for application in ordinary life.

Exercise in Reception #1: Remembering a Good Sermon

Over the years, churchgoers will have heard hundreds of sermons—both good and bad. Sometimes one will reach out and speak directly to your life. To reflect on the impact of preaching in your life, take a moment to remember a sermon that held a message of special importance to you. Can you recall who was preaching, and what he or she said? Perhaps a sentence or two were particularly meaningful, and have remained in your mind ever since.

Take a moment to recall a particularly meaningful sermon before you read on.

For most church members, sermons are the major source of ongoing religious education, and they can be an excellent source indeed. Good sermons are often directly relevant to the working world. One priest spoke on Labor Day of the need to value the work of men and women, and to carefully evaluate technology which eliminates jobs. He made the point that increasing profits by forcing more and more of the labor force into unemployment would eventually undermine both the economy and the spirit of the worker. A woman deacon preached one Sunday about the anguish of a policeman who had accidentally killed a young girl while on patrol, and she spoke of how Jesus can heal life's greatest hurts and bring wholeness to broken hearts.

If you approach a member of the clergy with the question about how to allow the Gospel into your life, you will almost certainly be given a warm and helpful response. But there are some limitations because the professional minister usually lives in a world centered around the church. You may or may not believe that a minister who has spent a career working in the church could really understand how things work in "the real world."

In truth, some do and some don't. Just as physicians can recognize and treat diseases they themselves have never had, some pastors can give remarkably insightful direction in a business world they have never entered. Even so, most clergy do not provide organized ministry to people in the working world, and much more could be done. The specific and practical issues of business life, the often spirit-crushing demands of the capitalist main stream, seem to require a different type of guidance and support than most local churches are able to provide.

A few clergy have initiated programs for men and women trying to live their Christian lives in the workplace. Yet one woman editor living in New York City went to an early morning meeting for "Christians in the Marketplace" only to find that it was exclusively for men! What's needed is effort combined with enough vision to see past such limited horizons. Why don't you try to convince your local clergy to develop a study group or a special ministry team or develop such a group yourself?

The third group in the church is the laity, the ordinary men and women who make up the vast majority of church membership. Working Christians are often storehouses of knowledge and useful wisdom, with a practicality far beyond that found in the statements of denominational bodies or even in the best of sermons. Unfortunately, they rarely share their knowledge with each other because they believe the denomination or the pulpit is responsible for the Christian message in the working world. They forget that *they* are the Christian message in the working world.

The laity, yourself included, is out there in the working world. You are not as easily identifiable as ministers with clerical collars or nuns in their habits, but you are there. You and your brothers and sisters of the laity are the church, as much as any pastor or member of the State Board of Elders. You must learn to minister to each other because no one else fully understands the challenges and joys of following Jesus in the bustling marketplace. There are three steps that will open up your own experience of and participation in the ministry of the laity in the working world.

First, recognize that being faithful to the Gospel at work is an important part of church life. The pews on Sunday contain many men and women who take church seriously, but who are so deeply involved in their business and community activities that they don't have the time or the interest to run the Mission Board or the Thursday Night Bingo. Nonetheless, they struggle to live their Christianity in the offices and factories and social agencies where they work. In doing so, they take the good news into the real world. The activities of the denominational body and the clergy are meant to support the most important activity of all—following Jesus in your daily life.

Second, break out of your invisibility. Remember, the followers of Jesus are unusual people in the business world, and a lot of people understandably keep their faith a secret at work. You can only come together when you recognize each other. And the only way to recognize each other is to make your presence—as a Christian—known.

Just let out the secret. Mentioning the church, or Christianity, in any small positive way, tells the others present that you take the church seriously. A sermon in the office lounge or the nursing station is rarely necessary or appropriate. But, if you mention church sometime when it isn't expected, such as at a staff meeting or on a coffee break—''I saw the game Sunday after I got home from church"—everybody will know of your faith. The "secret" will be out. The nonbelievers will watch you with a new interest, and the other Christians will know that you stand with them.

Some people like to proclaim their faith in a very pushy way. Faith is a wonderful thing, and it ought to be shared, but some do it in ways that communicate a sense of moral superiority and a palpable self-satisfaction. It is one thing to be open about your faith, and quite another to preach about it in the corridors. More people will be attracted by the quiet witness of a truly loving person than by the Bible-thumping harangues of an amateur evangelist.

Exercise in Reception #2: Letting Out the Secret

Imagine yourself simply mentioning the church at your job, in passing and without preaching. This might be old hat for you, or it may be a completely new experience. What might you say to gently make your faith known?

Before you read on, imagine letting out the secret.

Once the secret is out, people will look at you differently, and the other members of the laity will know that you are there. Remember, many of them are silent as well, and you may have no idea who they are. By simply expressing your faith you may give hope and comfort to those who share your journey.

The third step requires you to actively seek out other Christian men and women who work at jobs similar to your own. You may not know people in your own congregation who are in your line of work. Those contacts will have to be sought out. When you quietly state your belief on the job, others may tell you that they are also Christians.

If you find someone who would like to get together and talk, be sure to follow up. You might want to set up a lunch date or an evening get together, but make it clear in advance that you would like to talk about your common experience of trying to live the Gospel at work. Something greater is called forth in the simple act of getting together. Whether you are fire fighters, border patrol officers, or bank loan managers, nobody knows the risks and opportunities of your particular job like a fellow professional. And whatever your job, a unique perspective is gained by discussing work with a colleague who is also trying to follow Jesus on the job.

There are several possibilities for sharing. You might just want to have lunch together now and then and talk about your work, all the while acknowledging that you are getting together *because* of your shared faith—even if you don't always discuss it directly. You may want to seek the perspective of another Christian on specific decisions you face at work or on situations that come up constantly on the job. You and the other lay man or woman may want to pray together. Some people are comfortable with shared prayer and others find it painfully difficult. You may study the Bible together, or reflect on a recently published church document, or call the pastor and suggest forming a support or study group for working men and women.

Remember, nobody on earth understands your work experience like another person with a similar job. Someone who does work like yours is uniquely competent to make practical, realistic suggestions on facing its challenges.

Finally, when two Christians come together, others may well hear about it and want to join them. In many cities there are formal and informal support groups which offer sharing and fellowship in the journey of faith. What starts out as a lunch for two may grow into a regular meeting for seven or eight, offering shared experiences, wisdom, and pain.

The church is necessary in the Christian's working life. The challenges of the bustling marketplace make the support and guidance of the church essential for the followers of Jesus. Each of the three groups, the denominational body, the local clergy, and the laity, offers its own strengths and resources. As members of God's family, working for a living, we need all the help we can get. That help is available only in the church.

If we live by the truth and in love, we shall grow in all ways into Christ, who is the head by whom the whole body is fitted and joined together, every joint adding its own strength, for each separate part to work according to its function. So the body grows until it has built itself up, in love. (Ephesians 4:15-16)

9

Learning to Think Like a Christian: Component Seven— Sharing Your Decisions with God in Prayer

SUPPOSE YOUR COMPANY NEEDS PARTS, AND YOU ARE responsible for placing the order by Thursday of this week. They can be purchased from a local firm or for 38 percent less from a Latin American supplier. Buying Latin American would mean better profits for your stockholders and lower expenses for the firm. However, the local company may be facing layoffs and need the work. But the Latin Americans might need work, too, and while laid-off American workers get unemployment checks, unemployed Latin Americans are often reduced to levels of extreme poverty. The decision is troublesome and the answers aren't clearcut.

What do you do with the parts order?

Serious-minded working people inevitably face situations where action is demanded and the best possible choice is not self-evident. Should one press for a promotion that would mean more money but less time with the family? Should one work for a company that makes atomic weapons or profitably imports clothing produced by children laboring in Asian sweatshops? Perfect answers to these questions do not rush to mind or jump from the pages of the Scriptures.

If two or three Christians were talking about a vexing problem and one of them said, "You should pray over the decision," that would be a good suggestion. But what would that really mean? There is considerable unexpressed confusion about what it means to pray for guidance and what sort of response one ought to expect from God. Some people regularly pray for instruction and wisdom, while others try it now and then but often feel confused and even a bit disappointed if their prayers don't provide them with clear—and painless—solutions.

Exercise in Recollection #1: Do You Pray
for Guidance?

Can you remember a *specific* situation when you prayed for moral guidance at work? Take the time to search your memory for an actual instance.

Once you recall the specific instance, try to remember what happened. Did you feel like you received God's guidance? How did you know?

Before reading on, spend a moment recalling
a specific time when you prayed for moral guidance
at work.

People have different expectations when praying for guidance. The Christian's moral goal is to follow the will of God, and no one would be surprised to hear a sermon on that theme. The preacher says, "You've got to let Jesus take control of your life" or "The fullest realization of self lies in doing the will of God." On a theoretical level, that is a clear message, but its practical applications are not easily specified. Christians

98

have struggled for centuries with the task of discerning the will of God in specific situations. For the problem presented at the beginning of this chapter, the prayer might be, "What do you want me to do with this parts order, Jesus?"

Is prayer a "pipeline" through which God dictates specific and detailed instructions for daily life? This is an important question because it forces us to examine the nature and purpose of prayer. Can you say, "Hey, God, I've got a problem" and expect Him to respond, "OK, here's the solution: call the purchasing department and tell them that on Friday . . ."? If this were the way it worked, there would be no reason to make moral decisions by any other means. If God regularly gave specific directives to ordinary working people, it would be stupid or sinful (or both!) to do anything other than ask God for orders and follow them to the letter.

Prayer, understood as a pipeline, is a request for an unambiguous personal revelation of the will of God, over and above what is available in the Scriptures. It is as though one were asking to hear the voice of God. That experience is hardly unknown in the Scriptures, especially in the Old Testament. Adam, Moses, Samuel, Elijah, Isaiah, and others heard God speak to them plainly and directly. God told them what to do and how to do it. And others received instructions in dreams or from angels.

Only rarely is the voice of God reported in the New Testament. It is heard at the Baptism and Transfiguration of Jesus, by Paul on the road to Damascus, and in the Revelation of John, all decidedly unusual incidents. The Holy Spirit occasionally gives directives in the book of Acts and there are a few appearances in the New Testament of angels who carry explicit instructions for action.

Some qualities of God's direct messages are worth noting. First, in the New Testament they don't seem to come because people ask for them; such revelations occur strictly on God's initiative. Peter was concerned with finding some lunch when a vision overtook him (Acts 10:9–21), and he was still pondering the vision's significance when the Spirit came to him again to tell him what it had meant. Similarly, Paul was certainly not asking for advice from Jesus when he was knocked off his horse on the road to Damascus. The New Testament does not suggest that one can expect a direct revelation from God just by asking for it. In fact, quite the opposite appears to be true. (2 Peter 1:19–21)

A second quality of such direct messages is that they are fairly rare, both in the New Testament and in the lives of Christians today. The clear and unmistakable message from God is heard occasionally though, and the history of Christianity contains many instances of saints who experienced the direction of God in vivid ways. When God does break in on human life, it is a truly miraculous event. But in our daily lives and those of the ordinary people in the Bible, such miraculous personal revelation does not seem very common.

There is a third problem with personal revelation: the dangerous risk of self-deception. You can insist that an idea of yours is the personally revealed will of God. No one, then, had better question it. Such a sense of proof in the heart can lead to smugness and an inability to consider other points of view. Quite honestly, you may be flatly wrong.

One of the authors, a clinical psychologist, has met a fair number of people who were absolutely sure that the voice of God had told them to kill people or to commit suicide. Those voices had more to do with their psychopathology than with direct communication from God. However, no logic would convince those unfortunate people of that fact.

Another time one of us was sitting in a prayer meeting of devout Christians who were trying to find a solution to a difficult issue that had been raised. All at once he became certain that the answer to the group's problem was held in Mark 17:20. The chapter and verse were so clear, he "knew" that this must be a "word of wisdom," a moment of revelation. Eagerly he sought the verse in his Bible and found that Mark has only sixteen chapters. Direct personal revelation must be measured by the Scriptures and the insights of other believers. Otherwise there is simply too much opportunity to fool yourself and blame your foolishness on God.

The voice of God is seldom heard. The working of the Spirit, the guiding power of God, appears to function most often in a gentler, less dramatic way. But if you're expecting drama, gentleness can be overlooked.

The following is a joke told in elementary school playgrounds all across the nation. It was raining, and Jake lived on low ground. A man came by; "You'd better get out of here, there's going to be a flood." "I'm not worried," replied Jake, "God will save me." The river rose, and Jake had to go up to the second floor. A lifeboat came by, but Jake sent them away. "God will save me." Soon he had to climb out on the roof. Another lifeboat came, but he wouldn't get in. Finally Jake was treading water, clinging desperately to his TV antenna. A helicopter came and started to lower a rope. "Go away," shouted Jake, "God will save me." Just then the antenna gave away and Jake drowned. A while later, in heaven, he confronted God. "Why didn't you save me?"

"Jake," responded the Lord, "I sent a man, two lifeboats, and a helicopter. What more do you want?"

Sometimes we get an idea of what we want God to do, and then we don't notice Him when He does something else. If you are expecting explicit instructions, you may miss guidance that comes in other ways. But if prayer is not usually a pipeline for directions from God, what are you supposed to expect? If you aren't likely to hear God's voice or see His finger writing on the wall, what guidance does prayer offer?

God is both present and absent, active in the world and yet apart from it. His existence is beyond human comprehension. How does He communicate His will? How do you figure out what He wants done? In the spe-

101

cific terms of our example, how does God send messages about what one should do with the parts order?

Instructions on demand would be nice. Why not? From a practical point of view it would take care of all our problems. But our review of Scripture and human experience indicates that this is not the common nature of return communication in prayer.

Throughout the Bible the writers of Scripture use the analogy of God as light. A few examples will give some sense of the power of that comparison.

Now your word is a lamp to my feet, a light on my path. (Psalm 119:105)

The people that lived in darkness have seen a great light; on those who dwell in the land and shadow of death a light has dawned. (Matthew 4:16)

The Word was the true light that enlightens all men; and he was coming into the world. (John 1:9)

On these grounds is sentence pronounced; that though the light has come into the world men have shown they prefer darkness to the light because their deeds were evil. And indeed, everybody who does wrong hates the light and avoids it, for fear his actions would be exposed; But the man who lives by the truth comes out into the light, so that it may be plainly seen that what he does is done in God. (John 3:19–21)

You were darkness once, but now you are light in the Lord; be like children of light, for the effects of the light are seen in complete goodness and right living and truth. (Ephesians 5:9–10)

This is what we have heard from him, and the message that we are announcing to you: God is light; there is no darkness in him at all. If we say that we are in union with God while we are living in darkness, we are lying because we are not living the truth. But if we live our lives in the light, as he is in the light, we are in union with one another, and the blood of Jesus, his son, purifies us from all sin. (1 John 1:5)

Exercise in Recollection #2: Instructions in a Dark Room

Imagine being locked in a totally dark room. The key, unknown to you, is on a nail which hangs between two framed pictures above an overstuffed chair. If you can grope around and find the key, and then manage to locate the door, you will be free. But remember, you don't know there is a key—all you know is that you're stuck.

Now imagine that a mysterious voice tells you how to find the key and get to the door. You are now able to leave. This solves the immediate problem, but you don't know much more about the room and if you are ever back there with another problem to solve, you will have to wait for instructions again.

Now, imagine yourself back in the room, but with the lights on. You can see the key and the door and everything else in the room as well. You may decide to leave immediately or to stay and explore. You may notice a staircase leading up to another interesting room. You still have to figure out what to do, but unlike before, you now have the information needed to solve the problems and go on.

Consider the analogy of prayer answered with light before you read on.

The answer to prayer is often more like light than a voice. God turns on the lights, opening our eyes to the possibilities of the situation, and permits us to choose.

It is not accidental that the writers of the Scriptures chose light as an image to represent God. We rarely notice light. Instead, we see objects which are made visible by it. Right now you see the pages of a book. Or at least you think you see them. In fact your eyes see only the light reflected from the book. We don't think about light at all until there is no longer enough to see by. Like God, light is paradoxical—it is invisible, and yet it is the only thing we can see.

Also, one cannot look directly at the source of a bright light. One can be blinded by looking into the sun or the filament hotly glowing in a strong lamp. The source of light, like light itself, is visible and yet invisible, while everything else is made visible because of its presence.

And finally, "light," God's light, cannot make your decisions for you. It can give you new information, but you still must decide for yourself. Even with the aid of its illumination people can still make mistakes—you may decide to sit and cry instead of looking for the key on the wall or you may even close both your eyes to the light and keep praying for a voice—but that is not the fault of the light.

A person hoping for a voice may be disappointed by light because it isn't what he had in mind. But rather than opening a pipeline for specific instructions, prayer for guidance appears to be answered most often with light. The answer to prayer is usually not a ready-made, prepackaged plan of action from heaven. Rather, God opens our eyes to the possibilities of love. He grants a renewed awareness of His love, and of our oneness with every brother and sister on this planet. He calls forth

104

new impulses of love and allows us to discern the possibilities for expressing that love in the present situation.

It is a bit presumptuous of us to offer an exercise on how to pray for guidance. It is like telling people how to become wise, and we run the risk of setting up the superstitious notion that if you follow a given formula, God will automatically illuminate the decision-making process. God cannot be manipulated in that fashion. If you decide to try this exercise, please do so knowing that it is neither magical nor "right" in any special sense. It is an experiment from which you may be able to learn.

Exercise in Recollection #3: Abiding with Your Decision

This exercise will take a while. You may want to do it right now or later, when more time is available. Choose a specific, difficult work-related decision to consider in prayer. Think about it before praying about it. Try to review all of its difficulties and complications. In other words, worry it over for a while.

When you are ready to pray, begin by entering a prayerful attitude. Do this in whatever way is your custom—you may kneel or sit, or begin by saying the Lord's Prayer or by just emptying your mind. It is important to undertake this prayer without any expectations about what will come from it. You will enter a double trap if you have a specific result in mind. You may conjure up your solution out of a desire for it to occur, or your concentration on what you want may prevent you from noticing what you actually receive. So be attentive, be open, and don't try too hard.

Let the decision to be made or the problem to be solved come into your mind. And then, mentally, take the problem and hold it in your hands. Raise it up to God. And just sit there with it. Abide with the problem. Don't try to solve it; don't move the elements

105

about looking for a missing key; don't try to escape from the anxiety it may cause. Just sit there with the problem and with God.

Your mind will try to solve the problem in its accustomed way, so solutions are bound to crop up. Let them go, and abide some more. Notice what comes into your head, but don't cling to any of it. If you find yourself paying attention as your thoughts run back and forth, looking for a solution, calculating the odds of this or that idea working out well, pull out of the analysis and don't get involved. Let the thoughts go as soon as you notice them. Know that if there are words in your mind, they are almost certainly your own words. Turn back to God. Wait. Sit with the problem a while longer.

And when you have done this for a comfortable period of time, stop. Notice what has happened, reflect on what has occurred, and go on with your day.

Before you read on, take time to pray about a difficult work-related decision or think about when you might have time to do so.

Prayer for guidance, done in this manner, opens you to God's presence. There may not be immediate "results," but your thinking is likely to be vulnerable to new viewpoints. When God is present He brings light. It may be that you find a new light, a light which was not there before.

What are you supposed to do with the parts order? The answer is probably not on the way down the pipeline of prayer, but there is plenty of light if you seek it. God's love may open possibilities you have not even considered. You may order from your neighbor, or from Latin America. You may decide to split the order, or set up a committee at work to consider in depth the ethics of your purchasing decisions. You may decide that the order is not the most important issue, and that you are called to become involved directly in the pursuit of social justice in Latin America or in your hometown.

In the light of God, we still make human, fallible choices. Pray for God to open your eyes to His light, and then decide with humility, knowing that the decisions, and the responsibility remain your own.

When Jesus spoke to the people again, he said: "I am the light of the world; anyone who follows me will not be walking in the dark; he will have the light of life." (John 8:12)

• 10 •

Deciding Now:
Choosing Christian Action

I N THE OLD TESTAMENT, THE CRITICAL DECISION FOR
the individual was whether or not to follow the Law.
To the gathered people of Israel, Moses stated its claims:

> See, today I set before you life and prosperity, death
> and disaster. If you obey the commandments of Yah-
> weh your God that I enjoin on you today, if you love
> Yahweh your God and follow his ways, if you keep
> his commandments, his laws, his customs, you will
> live and increase, and Yahweh your God will bless
> you in the land which you are entering to make your
> own. (Deuteronomy 30:15-17)

In contrast, the Gospel does not call one to follow a
list of "commandments, laws and customs," but to follow a person, Jesus, the Son of God. The critical choice
for the Christian is whether or not to follow the path of
Jesus.

Matthew was a businessman who collected Roman
taxes and kept a handsome share for his efforts. Jesus

called Matthew while he was at work. Matthew's response is a model for all Christians.

As Jesus was walking on from there he saw a man named Matthew sitting by the customs house, and he said to him, "Follow me." And he got up and followed him. (Matthew 9:9)

Jesus called and Matthew followed. Jesus made Himself known to Matthew and Matthew decided to go with Him.

The preceding chapters have discussed the process of learning to think like a Christian. Paul said that we had to conform our minds to that of Jesus. His words, "In your minds you must be the same as Christ Jesus" point to the long-range goal of your decision to stand up and follow Jesus.

If you think like a Christian you permit Jesus to make Himself known in your life. Thinking like a Christian means learning to listen for His call, wherever you are. Jesus is always there, directing the way to a new life—but you have to listen.

From Christian thinking grows Christian action. Matthew stood up and followed Jesus. Paul, knocked from his horse by a vision of the risen Lord, immediately set off to preach the Gospel. Neither sat around and pondered the experience—they went right to work. They began by doing the things that made the presence of Jesus a visible reality.

Those who actually hear the call also follow. The intention to take His path is lived out in the large and small choices we make every day. Matthew was at work by the customs house, collecting taxes. In Luke's Gospel, it is said that ". . . leaving everything, he got up and followed him." (Luke 5:28) Having heard the call of Jesus, that particular businessman started living differently.

But what are you to do starting on Monday? Having heard the call, how are you to follow? There is no single answer, no ready formula, no list of "commandments, laws and customs'' for the working Christian. No one can say how you should follow because no one can know what Jesus is calling you to do. The decisions you face on the job, the opportunities or dangers encountered when you next go to work, are individual to you. This much is sure: Jesus will be there with you, and if you let Him, He will put you to work building His kingdom. But no one can know what work He will have for you to do.

The Christian's moral task is to listen for the call of Christ and discern its direction. This is a very different process than that of our usual decision making. The classic American model for business decisions is the Harvard case study method. In this method one defines the central problem, lists relevant factors, outlines alternative courses of action with their anticipated advantages and disadvantages, analyzes the relative merits of each alternative, draws conclusions, and makes the decision. This method or one very much like it is taught in every business school in America. Its use leads one to be more methodical and logical, but it does not ordinarily allow for input from Jesus in the process.

We will now present a step-by-step procedure for thinking about moral decisions from a particularly Christian viewpoint. This procedure draws upon the components of Christian thinking presented in earlier chapters. For that reason, the exercise will prove much more profitable for those who have given time and effort to the previous chapters' instruction.

Step One: Take Time to Think

You need to think before acting. That sounds absurdly simple, but people have a number of ways of avoiding thinking about their decisions.

Some jump into action without thinking at all. Vexing choices make people anxious and some individuals end the discomfort by quickly *doing something*. These people often find that they have made up their minds without giving their problems sufficient thought. They find themselves implementing solutions *before* hearing what the problem is all about.

Others avoid thinking about their choices by staying busy with tasks unrelated to the problem at hand. They nervously pursue irrelevant odd jobs, such as cleaning all the wrenches or making sure 400 floppy disks are arranged in tidy numerical order. This is classic stalling and is wholeheartedly undertaken so as to avoid making decisions.

Taking time to think is not to stall. It means actually setting aside a quiet period to consider the decision, to ponder what ought to be done. A few minutes set aside to seriously contemplate a decision will lead to a sounder choice than that to be reached by leaping at the first solution that comes to mind.

The key is deciding to decide. Say to yourself, "Right now, I'm going to spend some time thinking about this problem, and I'm going to make a decision." Try to have a clear idea of how much time you should give to the problem. The decision may require ten minutes or three hours, yet even a minimum of two or three minutes can break you of the habit of jumping into action without adequate reflection. By the same token, telling yourself that "This is the time to decide" may end years of chronic stalling.

Set the stage for your decision making. It helps to have some paper and a pencil as tools. (The notebook introduced in the chapter on reason and experience is perfect for this use.) Do nothing else during the decision-making time. Sifting through the mail or glancing at the T.V. set while thinking about a complex problem will almost certainly distract you and make it easy for you to stall.

You may discover that more information is needed, or that others should be consulted before you can make a sound choice. Set a time line, a preset date when the information will be available and the decision can be made. Deciding to wait is not the same as stalling. Going to the supervisor for specific information is different from going to him to chat and so avoid making the decision.

111

Step Two: Write at Least One Complete Sentence
that Identifies the Decision You Need to Make

Suppose your organization is forced into a budget reduction by a slowdown in the economy. You are charged with reducing personnel expenses. Your union agreement provides for two alternatives: laying off the four most recently hired employees or reducing the insurance benefits for the twelve people on the management team.

It is tempting to forget about the problem and put the personnel files in alphabetical order. But you decide to tackle the problem, and set aside an hour to really think it through to a conclusion. The first thing you do in that hour is write down one or two sentences about the decision to be made at the top of a piece of paper or a notebook page. You should be as concrete and specific as possible, and put down only enough to plainly state the issue.

I need to decide whether to lay off the last four union people we hired or to reduce the life insurance and early retirement benefits for the management staff.

Writing the issue down helps in a number of ways. First, it focuses the mind on the need for a decision. Second, it prevents the mind from wandering away to easier but less important decisions, such as whether or not to renew the contract with the window washing company or what color paper to use for the staff newsletter. Lastly, it prepares the mind to deal effectively with the problem at hand. Writing sets wheels turning in the higher centers of the brain, and the simple act of thinking through and writing down even one or two *complete sentences* can bring into clear focus what may have been lost in rambling, emotional worry.

Taking the time to write down the issue in a complete sentence can even help you deal more effectively with small decisions. And, if you have only three minutes to

112

make a choice, spend part of that time writing down the decision you need to make. It will help you.

These first two steps are quite general. At this point, however, we take a radical turn. The remaining steps are specifically designed to help bring Christian preparation to bear on job decisions. They are meant to open you to the call of Christ, and not necessarily to make you rich.

Step Three: Accept Responsibility for Making the Decision

There is no way to escape responsibility for making decisions, so face the responsibility squarely. The decision is yours to make, and the Gospel demands that you look for and follow the direction of Christ.

Take a moment, after writing down the decision to be made, to reflect on the fact that it is really *your* decision. Even if you decide to let somebody else choose the final course of action, it is your decision *not* to make the decision yourself. A good way to acknowledge this responsibility is to read what you have written, and say inwardly, "This is my decision to make—and I am responsible to make it well."

Step Four: Remember the Presence of God

Remember that God is present while the decision is made. Matthew responded to Jesus' call, but in a way he had it easy. Jesus was standing right there, plainly visible and impossible to ignore. Remember that you also work alongside Jesus, even though He is not visible.

Too many small children have been terrified by their parents or teachers telling them, "Jesus is watching everything you do, so you'd better be good or else!" The adult reason for remembering God's presence is not to induce fear of doing bad things, but to draw out one's best choice. Remembering that He is there can help people find the courage to take the risk that following Him entails. Matthew, after all, did not merely repent of his

113

greed and promise not to cheat the Israelites quite so much. He stood up and walked away from a good business. Church tradition has long held that he died a martyr. The presence of Jesus gave Him the courage to make his best possible choice.

If you remember that you act in the presence of God you may find resources of hope and wisdom within yourself that you had not recognized before. If we listen, He calls us forth.

"Follow me."

Focus on the fact that you are making a decision in the presence of God, and that you are His co-worker. You might simply say, either silently or aloud, "Be with me, Lord, as I make this decision."

Step Five: Remember Your Neighbor, and
Your Responsibility to Serve

Jesus was definite about His commandment to love one another as He loved us. He sent every Christian to serve in love.

Think about the people who will be affected by your decision. It is a good idea to actually write down their names in your notebook. If you don't know their names, list the people by groups, but be sure to remember that these groups are made up of *REAL* people.

After making the list, try to imagine what the impact of your various options might be on those men and women. Write this down on your paper.

Any decision may affect as few as one or two people. Other decisions can have a direct impact on the lives of hundreds. Those people may be co-workers, customers, stockholders, or those who live near the manufacturing plants.

No matter how carefully you analyze the effects of a decision, you cannot predict all of the consequences. A laid-off employee might decide to go to law school and become mayor or go into business for herself and eventually buy out the company that fired her. Even if you try *very* hard, it is impossible to predict the outcome for each individual involved. But if you take the time to remember that those are all *real people*, and make an effort to consider the effects of your actions, you will be better equipped to bear in mind your Christian responsibility to serve them.

No computer program can come up with the "right" decision—even if all the variables are inserted and all the correct statistical analyses are applied. The future is beyond reliable human or mathematical prediction. But Jesus calls you to love and to serve. Too many people make their decisions based on one consideration—what will this do for me? By remembering the needs of the other men, women, and children involved in your decision, you will open your mind to possibilities which might otherwise have been missed.

Step Six: Apply Reason and Experience

The first step here is to reflect on whether this decision is dealt with in the ethical codes of your profession. Have serious men and women thought about this sort of situation before and written down what they learned from experience?

For example, if a counselor discovered that a colleague of his was involved in a sexual relationship with a patient, the way would be clear. The ethical codes of virtually every organized group of therapists prohibit sexual activity between a therapist and his client. The counselor's professional organization would have clear guidelines on how to handle situations of misconduct by a colleague.

If your decision is handled by the ethical code for your group, it behooves you to recall this fact *before* making a decision. It helps to be familiar with the code.

The second step is to recall whether or not you have made similar decisions in the past. If you have, try to recall what you decided to do then. What were the effects of that decision on others? Was something learned in that earlier situation that could be applied here? If you have been keeping a notebook, you may be able to find notes which can shed light on the present choice.

Step Seven: Look for Direction in Scripture

You may be able to find a story from Scripture that resembles your predicament. Remember, the deepest and most comprehensive form of Scriptural morality is the imitation of Christ. Christ's teaching, and His example, are the ultimate standard for all of your daily decisions.

One of the authors is a former Veteran's Administration social worker. He spent years counseling Los Angeles's down-and-out vets. During that time, it always seemed that his clients would call him, broke and hungry, about to be thrown out of their hotel rooms at ten minutes till five every Friday night. They were invariably in those situations because they had failed to plan ahead or because somebody in the V.A. had lost their paperwork. In either case, the problem was not the author's fault and it was time for him to go home.

At those times, he recalled our Lord's story of the Good Samaritan and asked himself if tonight he was going to be the Levite, the priest, or the Samaritan who offered assistance. Often, although not always, remembering our Lord's example, he would take the time to help.

Reflecting on Scripture is fruitless if you only want rules. Instead, seek out examples of loving service. Christian morality grows out of a loving response to the God who loves us and who gave us Jesus as our finest example of service. The more the Scriptures become your own story, the more you will be able to recall and follow their examples of love in action.

Step Eight: Seek Guidance from the Church

You may be able to recall some helpful point of teaching or doctrine from the writings of Christian ethicists and theologians. Likewise, you may remember something your pastor said during a sermon or in a meeting which applies to the choice at hand. Take time to search your memory for such guidance.

If there is enough time, you may decide to discuss the decision with other Christians who hold jobs similar to your own. This alternative takes you out of the realm of an immediate decision. However, if the problem is complex, you can profitably draw from the insights of others. Remember the importance of the laity in the working world, and allow another working Christian to minister to you.

Step Nine: Share the Decision with God in Prayer

At this point you have completed the first eight steps, and a great deal of information is competing for space in your mind. Solutions are suggesting themselves, and you may have already begun to make a decision.

Now is the time to pray for the light of God's guidance. Take the decision, along with all the other ideas in your head, and offer them as prayer, in whatever way is most comfortable for you. You may want to mentally take the problem, hold it in your hands, and raise it up to God. However you pray, abide with the problem, and know that though God will not send an angel from heaven with the right answer, He will offer you light and so illuminate your decision. Let your mind become open to possibilities not seen before.

Sometimes you will become aware of a new vision of the problem—God's light can be very clearly present. Other times it may seem that "nothing happened." Remember that nothing spectacular is supposed to happen—prayer is hardly ever accompanied by mystical fireworks, no matter how much they are desired. And don't feel bad if there aren't any specific instructions from God. He gives light, not notes. Look for the light, and go on.

Step Ten: Decide, and Share Your Decision with Jesus

At some point in this process you will make a decision. One choice will seem more appropriate than the others, and you will feel ready to begin action. Sometimes the right choice will become evident to you very early in the process, during the first few steps. But go through each of the steps. Even a brief walk through may help you avoid leaping too quickly into action. Other times, though, reviewing every item on the list won't provide you with a clean, immediately evident answer to the problem. The hardest decisions are those where none of the choices is plainly correct. When each of the available options presents difficulties, no choice can be made without some regret. In those cases, one still needs to decide and a time limit will help prevent unproductive stalling.

When you have recognized what appears to be the best choice, write down your decision and, again, be specific. It is also a good idea to make a few notes on what factors led to your decision. As we pointed out in Chapter 6, those notes will later provide new opportunities for learning.

Finally, share your decision with Jesus, acknowledging that it is a step in your journey of faith. "This is my decision, Jesus. I am trying to follow where you lead me."

Each time you go through this process, you learn more about making Christian decisions, about discerning the call of Jesus. It may seem that it could be done faster by skipping some of the steps—and it could. However, it is important to master the process and the only way to do so is to go through every step. The method is similar to that of the teacher who makes the entire class—even those who know the answer—repeat the lesson. Only in this way does the process become comfortable and fluid for you.

In some instances, you will have plenty of time for studying relevant Scripture or discussing the issues in detail with other Christians. Taking that time is not only sound decision making, it is a good way to study and learn with Jesus as your co-worker.

However, other decisions must be made more quickly; deadlines must be met. You still need to take time to think, though, even if little time is available. And it still helps to write down a sentence or two about the decision. Moving quickly through the list of steps, reflecting for a few seconds on each step, will help you respond to more than the pressures of the moment.

Step One: Take time to think

Step Two: Write at least one complete sentence that identifies the decision you need to make (even if you are in a hurry!)

Step Three: Accept responsibility for making the decision yourself

Step Four: Remember that you are in the presence of God

Step Five: Remember your neighbor, and your responsibility to serve

Step Six: Apply reason and experience

Step Seven: Look for direction in Scripture

Step Eight: Seek guidance from the church

Step Nine: Open the decision to God in prayer

Step Ten: Decide, and share your decision with Jesus

If you have genuinely made the commitment to go with Jesus, like Matthew you will stand up and follow. When you have made your decision, act upon it, but act with humility. Any human decision may still be wrong, no matter how carefully you have reflected on the choice. And even if you have made the right choice, there is no particular reason to take special pride in it. The best decision is always a response called forth by God's love for you.

Christians cannot make their moral decisions by

searching for lists of composite rules. Paul told us that there is no salvation in the Law. Christian moral action consists of the believer following the call of Jesus and making His will a present reality in daily life. Christian morality is faith responding to love.

As Jesus was walking on from there he saw a man named Matthew sitting by the customs house, and he said to him, "Follow me." And he got up and followed him. (Matthew 9:9)

11

Competition:
Coming Out Ahead

Do not model yourselves on the behavior of the
world around you, but let your behavior change,
modelled by your new mind. This is the only way
to discover the will of God and know what it is that
God wants, what is the perfect thing to do.
(Romans 12:2)

Paul's challenge strikes us as unrealistic and impossible. The "world," after all, is everything we know. It is
our culture and society. It includes the songs we sing,
the games we play as little children, the TV shows we
watch, the way we talk to each other—everything around
us, including our business practices.

Just as one hardly notices the air unless it is polluted,
one rarely notices the world unless some part of it is
bothersome. Like the air, culture is part of the background, always there but rarely attended to.

Moral decisions cannot be made in a vacuum, unsul-
lied by the cultural patterns and attitudes of the world.

People make their decisions on the basis of deeply rooted assumptions about how they are supposed to relate to the life around them, assumptions which almost always go unexamined and unchallenged. They feel "normal," they "just make plain common sense," and they are accepted without question.

To do other than model yourself "on the behavior of the world," you must recognize the world for what it is. Our unspoken and unexamined ideas about the way people "normally" operate are a big part of what Paul meant by "the world." In this chapter and the next we will address two basic sets of attitudes about business life: the commonly held ideas about competition and the exercise of authority.

One of the most basic assumptions of American business life is that competition is both necessary and healthy. Few ideas are held with less critical attention than the idea that everybody ought to "go for the Brass Ring." The American idea of equal opportunity is joined with an unspoken assumption that the primary struggle is to get to the top first. The economic world is likened to a boarding house dinner table where too few potatoes have been served. Each individual must compete to get as much as possible. Some will have plenty, and others will go hungry. Each competes by the same rules, so the race is fair. The model holds that there will naturally be winners and losers. As long as the rules are just, the losers have only themselves to blame.

In this set of unchallenged assumptions, each individual is seen as a self-contained little capsule floating in the sea of economic life and obligated only to avoid unfairly restricting the other capsules or harming them on purpose. Other than these limits, there is little to encourage them to work beyond self-interest.

Classical economics, presented by writers such as Adam Smith, holds that competitive pursuit of self-interest in a free marketplace will lead to solutions to everyone's problems. The "invisible hand of the market'' will eventually produce the best possible outcome for society.

Whether or not competitive enterprise is the best way to achieve prosperity and fairness—a topic for debate in another forum—some very serious problems develop in a large and competitive society. If everybody is out to get to the top, then many will get pushed to the bottom. If I'm out to get mine, what happens to my obligation to love and serve you?

The results of such competition are pervasive. In one office, typists working on word processors had their work stored in a central computer. The computer kept track of each typist's output, and management offered prizes to those employees who typed the most lines each month. A problem arose, though. At first a paragraph here and there and then whole documents vanished from the electronic files. It wasn't an electronic mishap in the computer. One typist, pressed beyond her limits by the demanding competition, had turned to erasing the other typists' work, thereby reducing their line count. This was her desperate way to keep up and to be sure that she came out a winner.

The same effect can be seen on a global scale in the rise and fall of oil prices. At one point the oil producers were on top and knew it. Pursuing maximum profits, they ran prices up as fast as they could change the figures on their calculators. The impact on the rest of the world was to drive marginal companies out of business and cause a slowdown in the global economy. Eventually oil prices tumbled—who needs oil if your plants are closed? As prices fell, the producers became desperate and again competitively pursued self-interest, but in a different direction. In order to maintain sales, they competitively undercut each other, driving the prices so low that many oil-producing countries were no longer able to meet the interest payments on debts incurred when prices were high.

The Christian does not live by the standards of the

world. The Gospel challenges the world's general assumption that competition is normal, commonsensical, and the way people work. The two viewpoints are far apart.

Their resolution lies in allowing yourself to feel *uncomfortable* in the presence of Christ's teaching and example, a difficult and sometimes painful process. Christian faith is not a "warm fuzzy" designed to make you feel all cozy inside. That uncomfortable feeling which comes when you compare what you do with what Christ teaches is a sign of growth. To successfully gain perspective on the usual competitive model, use the characteristics of the early church, Koinonia and Shalom, as a standard to evaluate your relationships with others.

Koinonia is a very powerful Greek word used by Paul and other New Testament writers to express several different—and at first glance, unconnected—ideas. Koinonia is used to describe one's proper relationship with Christ (1 Corinthians 2:9), the nature of participation in the Lord's Supper (1 Corinthians 10:16), membership in the community of the church (Galatians 2:9, Acts 2:42), participation in Christ's death and resurrection (Philippians 3:10, 1 John 3:6,7), and finally, a monetary collection taken to support the poor (Romans 15:26, 2 Corinthians 8:4 and 9:3). Common translations into English include "community," "participation," and "distribution." No idea could be much further from our usual notion of economic competition.

Koinonia describes one of the primary qualities of Christian life. To be joined with Jesus is to be joined to each other. The Eucharist both produces community and is inseparable from community. This central act ties each Christian to the other members of the Body of Christ, our fellow believers, in visible and invisible ways. Paul stated it powerfully.

The blessing cup that we bless is a communion with
the blood of Christ and the bread that we break is a

communion with the body of Christ. The fact that there is only one loaf means that, though there are many of us, we form a single body because we all have a share in this one loaf. (1 Corinthians 10:16–18)

The same intimate relationship we have with Christ, expressed in the sharing of the bread and cup, makes us one body with each other. We strive to make this Koinonia a reality, not just in a spiritual sense, but in the real world as well. Koinonia is not a bland commitment to social pleasantness, a spiritual "Have a nice day." "We form a single body," says Paul. Could he possibly have meant that? Could people have really taken that idea seriously?

Scripture indicates that they took it very seriously indeed. The early church lived out Koinonia in practical ways. Its members shared their property, their money, and their lives, not just their good wishes. As Jesus shared a common purse with His disciples, so the Church in Jerusalem "held everything in common." (Acts 4:32) While its people retained some private property, they voluntarily pooled their resources, sacrificing individual abundance so that each would be able to have enough.

None of their members was ever in want, as all those who owned land or houses would sell them, and bring the money from them, to present it to the apostles; it was then distributed to any members who might be in need. (Acts 4:34,35)

Their example lent a force and power to their preaching. It was obvious to all that they took the newness of life seriously. The evidence in Scripture is clear and unambiguous: the early church sought to live as one body, to achieve Koinonia, with all its richness of meaning.

125

They did so because they had heard the words of Jesus. Christ announced the coming of God's kingdom, telling His hearers that the final age of the world was beginning in Him. The Jews knew that He meant the completion of the "messianic vision": the time foretold by the prophets, when swords would be turned into plowshares, when the poor and oppressed would no longer be trampled under foot, when all the world would enjoy God's peace—Shalom.

Like Koinonia, Shalom is a rich and meaningful word, implying not only a spiritual kingdom, but also the remaking of the world into a place where all have the chance to live a full and happy life. Shalom is not peace in the commonplace sense—"Nobody in our neighborhood is currently at war"—but rather a new world order where all share the bounty of God's creation, where justice and mercy replace self-centered motivations.

For the early church Koinonia and Shalom were not just pretty words to be passed back and forth during worship services. They were the goals of daily living. Goals give direction to behavior. In our competitive world, the "normal, common sense" goal is to get as much as possible for yourself. The Gospel sets forth different goals—Koinonia and Shalom.

The church as a body and you as a member of that body, are called upon to proclaim Christ's Kingdom of Koinonia and Shalom, of sharing and peace. You are supposed to live it, to act in ways that anticipate its final completion when the Lord will come in power and judgment. Jesus invited people to live in the Kingdom now, living not in competition but in loving community.

In one instance a spirit of competition arose among Jesus' followers. He resolved this conflict in a startling way.

Then the mother of Zebedee's sons came with her sons to make a request of him, and bowed low; and he said to her, "What is it you want?" She said to him, "Promise that these two sons of mine may sit one at your right hand and the other at your left in your kingdom." "You do not know what you are asking," Jesus answered. "Can you drink the cup that I am going to drink?" They replied, "We can." "Very well," he said, "you shall drink my cup, but as for seats at my right hand and on my left, these are not mine to grant; they belong to those to whom they have been allotted by my father." (Matthew 20:20–23)

Jesus knew the limits of His promise. He promised that Zebedee's sons could follow His path of sacrifice, that they could give themselves as He gave Himself. Beyond this He made no promises.

The people of Jesus' time wanted other assurances, and so do we. This can be seen in the the widespread and increasingly accepted American trend to portray Christianity as a functional tool to achieve individual success and prosperity. American Christians are tempted to believe that God is on their side in the economic competition. If you pray and are faithful to God, His payoff to you will be the next promotion, the next raise, or good luck in the stock market. You will win because you are a good Christian, and the other fellow will lose because he is not. The Gospel, in this view, is your guarantor of success in the competition. This viewpoint denies the central ideals of Koinonia and Shalom.

The contrast between the biblical vision and the ordinary way people look at things is disconcerting. It is easy to feel that God is pulling you in one direction while everything else is pulling you in another. Christian faith puts you in tension with the surrounding culture and at odds with its value system. It is difficult to live Koinonia and Shalom because they are so different from the usual competitive model of business and society.

Those of us who have been raised in the American

127

economic culture are well tuned to the idea of competing to get ahead. But Jesus thought His followers should relate to one another differently, and so did Paul and the members of the first church communities.

The Gospel and the world are often in opposition, and it is evident here. Seen through the prism of our culture, the Gospel is a recipe for economic suicide. Do the goals of Koinonia and Shalom mean that Christians are to renounce all positions of power and influence, to let the raises and promotions go to others because they withdraw from the race? Does being a Christian condemn you to being poor? Does it mean never striving to achieve high goals when more than one person wants the same thing?

The Gospel must be understood in terms that make sense in our culture but which remain faithful to Christ's vision. A balance must be struck. The Gospel cannot be diluted, but at the same time it must be connected with the complexities of economic life.

It is evident that some of the early Christians were people of wealth and high position. They were the ones who acted as hosts to the "house church" gatherings, the earliest worship services, and they were the patrons and supporters for the church's poorer members. How these people attained and held their positions in their society is not fully known. They may have competed to achieve their economic and social status, but they also lived lives that were very different from those of their non-Christian social and economic peers. The question "How could they, did they, do it?" remains and must be answered. How were they able to live the Gospel and still compete in their economic world?

Competition is not intrinsically a bad thing. When Paul used athletes as models for the self-discipline and intentness of purpose needed in Christian life, he said, "You must run in the same way, meaning to win." (1 Corinthians 9:24–27) The race was one of Paul's favorite images, and he used it repeatedly as an example for the steadfast striving the Gospel demands.

Competition which tears down the community is destructive. It can destroy relationships and evolve into a greedy striving for a success which makes Koinonia and Shalom impossibilities. Jesus left no room for the self-justification of people who prosper by stepping on others.

In his teaching he said, "Beware of the scribes who like to walk about in long robes, to be greeted obsequiously in the market squares, to take the front seats in the synagogues and the places of honour at banquets; these are the men who swallow the property of widows, while making a show of lengthy prayers. The more severe will be the sentence they receive." (Mark 13:38–40)

How do you compete in your own work life? It is important to look at your own competitive behavior by the Gospel standards of Koinonia and Shalom, sharing and peace. Competing for business, for customers, for positions of authority, is not in itself wrong. But you must consider the ways in which you compete and its effects on the community.

What is some current goal toward which you are striving at work? Take the time to let something specific come to mind, some end you would like to achieve. What are you seeking? Is it a promotion, an award in a sales competition, or recognition as the "best" in the department? Only you know what you really want. Let it come to mind.

Are you competing for that goal? Who are the other people who also want it? Can only one person get it, or can more than one share the goal? Sometimes goals are exclusive, and sometimes many can take part in them. If this is not a competitive situation, see if you can find a current example of competition in your work life.

Once you have identified some goal for which you are competing, there are several issues for reflection.

129

First, how much personal energy are you investing in the drive to achieve that goal? If it comes to mind over and over, at work and at home, it is very important in your life. Remember that the more important any goal becomes, the more it will be sought at the cost of other goals.

The most obvious example of this is what happens to family life when one member becomes overly invested in the competition at work. One spouse can let the marriage fall apart as he/she spends night after night working, striving to get ahead, struggling to reach some new plateau. If you find yourself repeatedly breaking commitments to your spouse or children because of work then you are out of balance. Your most intimate community of sharing, your family, can be eroded by your desire to get ahead.

This is a common experience. In fact, it is considered "normal," a necessary side effect of the effort to get ahead. In their recent book, *Top Executive Performance: 11 Keys to Success and Power*, William and Nurit Cohen mention the executive's family only once—in the section on "Sources of Stress." It is instructive that the book presents family life as a liability, as one more item on the busy business person's list of worries, rather than as a source of nurturance and support. When the goal of getting ahead becomes central, other things fall by the wayside, and that apparently includes the family. Unfortunately, the Cohens' book is far too typical; it reflects the "normal common sense" of the trend-setters in American competitive business life.

Second, the means you are willing to adopt in the competition must be examined. Have you ever bent your principles to get a competitive edge? Small items of personal deceit can have important implications. Think back over your pursuit of the recent goal. Did you occasionally "cheat" to get ahead of the competition? What people like to call "tricks of the trade" are often petty dishonesties, minor injustices. Spend some time thinking about

130

other instances when you might have stretched the truth or unfairly manipulated a situation to get ahead.

The enthusiasm and pressure of the race can lead you to do things you would not ordinarily consider. The problem with even little lies or tiny thefts is that they have a way of growing into bigger problems. Crossing an ethical line once makes it easier to cross over it again, exploring more of the territory each time.

If competition is leading you into a pattern of small compromises of ethics and values, be careful. When the opportunity comes along to move far ahead by doing something really crooked, your self-control may be out of practice.

The third issue is your relationship with the competition. It's easy to forget that even competitors share common interests. People often fall into competition out of habit when cooperation would be better for all involved.

In colonial New England, each town had some community-owned meadow land where all the town's farmers could graze their sheep. As long as each kept his flock at a reasonable size, the grass remained plentiful and all made a modest living. However, any individual farmer could increase the size of his flock and make a little bit more money. As long as the others didn't do the same thing at the same time, there was no problem, especially not for the farmer with the extra sheep. However, if everyone did increase the number of sheep they put to pasture, the grass soon became overgrazed and the common land barren. All the flocks went hungry.

The only escape is to recognize and respect your competitors' needs, and to learn to back away when necessary from your desire to always have more, to always be ahead. Community and peace, Koinonia and Shalom, should embody your Christian relationship with other competitors.

Often opportunities for cooperation are missed because of the habit of competition. At the local Swap Meet two booths used to sell discount cassettes of popular music. If a customer bought from one, he had less money

131

with which to buy from the other. The two merchants could have tried to undercut each other, but instead of competing, they have learned to cooperate. They now serve different customers, with one specializing in the teenage crowd and the other catering to those people who purchase jazz and foreign music. They have learned to keep their eyes open for bargains on tapes for each other and pass customers back and forth. The would-be purchaser knows that what one cannot provide, the other may have, and this increases the number of customers for both businessmen.

Similarly, two young executives don't need to compete. They may both be promoted faster if they work together successfully, rather than undercut each other's efforts. Sales representatives are likely to have more stable increases in their income if they cooperate, rather than jumping over one another to get the fast sale.

If you seek to cooperate rather than compete, will others treat you as well? Some will and some won't. You can only hope to lead by example. Again, Jesus places this one squarely on the believer's shoulders:

> So always treat others as you would like them to treat you; that is the meaning of the Law and the Prophets. (Matthew 7:12)

In Chapter 10 we presented a series of steps for choosing Christian action. Those steps apply to competitive situations as well. They will not be repeated here—you have read them once, and can refer to them when necessary. However, remember that the proper response of the Christian to the question, "What should I do now?" is always, "Whatever Jesus is calling you to do."

Being a Christian in the American marketplace means that you are a person in tension. Two sets of values, competition and getting ahead on one side, Koinonia and Shalom on the other, pull and tug at you, keeping you constantly off balance. The Christian must always keep the Gospel vision in mind.

Do not model yourselves on the behavior of the world around you, but let your behavior change, modelled by your new mind. This is the only way to discover the will of God and know what it is that God wants, what is the perfect thing to do. (Romans 12:2)

12

Being in Charge

JOBHOLDERS OCCASIONALLY THINK ABOUT BEING IN charge. As long as someone else is making the decisions it is easy to conclude that if you were the boss, the organization would hum along. Everybody second-guesses the one in charge, and many naturally believe that they could do a better job of calling the shots. Wouldn't we all love to have that corner office with the big windows!

It may come to pass that after years of griping about the people in charge, you move into management and become one of "them." Shortly after the self-congratulation ends, you will undoubtedly find that problems have accompanied your promotion. Perhaps the people in the shop aren't too enthusiastic about new ideas. Or the ones who look like "dead wood" have powerful allies in the higher levels of management and magical ways of evading all efforts to remove them. And finally, the staff is now griping about you. They all think they could do your job better if they only had the chance. You begin to realize why your predecessor retired early.

The difference between being a supervisor and being a worker is the exercise of authority. Jesus exercised authority, as the centurion of Capernaum recognized. Through some friends, he sent this message to Jesus:

"Sir," he said, "do not put yourself to trouble; because I am not worthy to have you under my roof; and for this same reason I did not presume to come to you myself; but give the word and let my servant be cured. For I am under authority myself, and have soldiers under me; and I say to one man: Go, and he goes; to another: Come here, and he comes; to my servant: Do this, and he does it." (Luke 7:6–9)

As a man who exercised authority, the centurion was accustomed to being in charge. He did not need to be present to see that his instructions were carried out because he expected obedience from his men. He also knew that his power was derived from the power of others: his general, the Roman governor, and finally, the Emperor. He was somewhere in the middle, answerable for his actions as others were answerable to him.

In any organization, somebody has to be in charge. No business, agency, or church can operate without someone making decisions. Large working groups cannot function if employees do whatever they feel like. Imagine the chaos in a hospital if the nurses wandered from floor to floor, looking for interesting things to do or if the surgeons came in whenever they felt like performing an operation. People are able to work together in groups because they submit to authority. Decisions are made about how things are to be done, and the people in the organization comply with them. In some places groups of workers make shared decisions about their tasks, but each employee must submit to the authority of the group decision. Workers need to know what their co-workers are going to do and their behavior in the workplace must be predictable. Without the exercise of authority, it would be impossible for people to work together successfully,

135

whether in hospitals, courthouses, or tire dealerships. It simply could not be done.

Authority is shared and delegated in many ways. In our government, decision makers are elected to make choices that the rest of us live by. Governmental authority, though, begins with the people. They grant it to their representatives. In business life, the basis of authority usually lies with the owners of the company. However, as soon as an organization has more than a few dozen employees, it becomes impossible for the owners to make all the everyday decisions. Sam Winston started a tire sales company that now operates over 150 stores in three states. He no longer decides who is going to work the Friday night shift at the Convoy Boulevard store. He and owners like him delegate their authority to executive officers, vice presidents, and cadres of managers, directors, team leaders, module coordinators, foremen, and supervisors.

The person who is promoted to a management position is delegated some portion of the owner's authority to make choices about who is to do what and how it is to be done. Like the centurion, he or she is probably someplace in the middle of the organization, with authority over some and under the authority of others.

Being in charge is an acquired skill. Any bookstore in America will offer you a startling variety of books on how to manage people. There are Theories X, Y, and Z, as well as Management By Objectives, Japanese Management, and Management Through Intimidation. Those books are big sellers, and it is no surprise. It is hard to get other people to do what you want them to do, in the way you want them to do it. From the manager's perspective, people function according to the Rule of Human Cussedness—"Given the chance, people will do whatever they darn well please." Getting them to do something else is a real challenge.

The centurion in the Gospel had some alternatives the modern American business manager cannot use. For example, if someone disobeyed orders, he could have the miscreant flogged or killed. Roman army units, if disobedient or cowardly in battle, could be decimated. Lots would be drawn, and the losers killed—one soldier in ten. That kind of power does not exist in our society, and few would like to see it introduced. However, a manager does direct behavior and so he has a few ways to punish those who refuse to comply with his orders. Uncooperative subordinates can be fired, reassigned to less attractive jobs, or denied raises.

A central issue for the Christian supervisor is how to handle this charge. Exercising authority is certainly an important part of responsible living, and nothing in the Gospel indicates that Christians should not use it. If God has granted you the skill and ability to lead and the opportunity to accept authority, you should not refuse those gifts. However, as a Christian, you are called to follow Jesus in all things—including the challenge of being boss.

Just as the Gospel forces Christians to reevaluate their deeply held ideas about competition, it also demands a careful reexamination of one's cultural expectations of authority. Starting with the basic Christian premise that Jesus was God among us, the entire story of His life and death and His remarkable teachings directly counter our "normal, common sense" ideas about being the boss.

Jesus was God's Son. All authority was His. And yet He set that all aside and entered human life in one specific time and place. The earliest record of Christ's life is found in Luke's Gospel. Luke notes that even before His birth, people knew that something special was happening. At His birth, angels sang joyfully in the countryside, announcing the coming of the Lord. And what is the first image we have of this God made man, this radical entry of the holy into human life?

> While they were there the time came for her to have her child, and she gave birth to a son, her first-born. She wrapped him in swaddling clothes and laid him in a manger because there was no room for them at the inn. (Luke 2:6–8)

137

The image of Jesus as a helpless infant is the first indication in the New Testament of God's way of exercising authority. In dealing with men and women, His totally dependent creatures, God set aside His power and assumed the form of a human baby. A baby without even a proper bed.

More than thirty years later, on the very last evening of His life on earth, Jesus knelt and washed the feet of His disciples. Over the protest of Simon Peter, who knew very well that servants washed the feet of their superiors, He insisted on this act.

> When he had washed their feet and put on his clothes again, he went back to the table. "Do you understand" he said "what I have done to you? You call me Master and Lord, and rightly; so I am. If I, then, the Lord and Master, have washed your feet, you should wash each other's feet. I have given you an example so that you may copy what I have done to you." (John 13:12–15)

The example of Jesus is made complete by His death. Though He possessed full authority and unlimited power He died helplessly on a cross. As Paul was later to write in his letter to the Philippians (2:5–11), Jesus did not cling to His equality with God but emptied Himself, taking on the form of a slave.

The Christian vision of authority is rooted in Jesus Himself. And that vision is a paradox. Here is what Jesus had to say about what should be expected of those in charge.

> The greatest among you must be your servant. Anyone who exalts himself will be humbled and anyone who humbles himself will be exalted. (Matthew 23:11)

> You know that among the pagans their so-called rulers lord it over them, and their great men make their

138

authority felt. This is not to happen among you. No; anyone who wants to become great among you must be your servant, and anyone who wants to be first among you must be slave to all. For the Son of Man himself did not come to be served but to serve, and to give his life as a ransom for many. (Mark 10: 41–45)

Jesus established a pattern that completely overturns the expected relationships. Some believe that He meant only to speak of how people should get along in the church. That is only partly true. Jesus was indeed talking about the church, and within the body of believers authority is to be exercised in a spirit of servanthood. But it is evident that Jesus never intended to establish two sets of norms, one for church use and one for all other situations. The thinking of the time simply could not allow for such segmentation of life, as we have pointed out at length in earlier chapters. Jesus did not direct His disciples to divide their lives into neat compartments with different rules for each.

Sadly, even the church has a history of failing to live up to Christ's standard. The first leaders of the church, the Apostles and Paul, exercised authority in a spirit of loving service. However, others have accepted power in the church but not the call to servanthood. These individuals use the church as a personal power base and serve only their desires for increased influence and control. It can be hard to tell such prelates and ministers from politicians or monarchs. If some individuals in the church find it difficult to be faithful to the Gospel vision, imagine how much harder is it for those in the business world to be faithful.

Business life fosters ambition and ambition can be self-serving. Jesus, and many writers of the Scripture, showed that authority used for any other purpose than service leads to corruption. The Scriptures are filled with examples of men and women who accepted responsibility and prospered and of those whose lust for power led to their downfall. In general, both the Old and New Testaments portray self-serving ambition as leading to sin, strife, and self-glory. The foremost example of Christ's response to the lust for power comes during the temptation in the desert.

> Then leading him to a height, the devil showed him in a moment of time all the kingdoms of the world and said to him, "I will give you all this power and the glory of these kingdoms, for it has been committed to me and I give it to anyone I choose. Worship me, then, and it shall all be yours." But Jesus answered him, "Scripture says: You must worship the Lord your God, And serve him alone." (Luke 4:5–8)

One can abuse the position of being the boss in a number of self-serving ways. First, authority can be used to procure for oneself the nicest office, the biggest desk, and first choice of vacation time. Perks and privileges come with being in charge, and it is not unusual to enjoy them and to quickly become accustomed to them. And since there is almost certainly somebody with a bigger desk, a better view, and a higher salary, there is almost always something more to want. Unfortunately, the boss can use the people he supervises as tools to get what he desires.

Second, people tend to treat the boss like a V.I.P. and it is tempting to believe that such treatment is owed you. The risk lies in thinking that you are somehow more valuable and important than the people you direct. Like the Pharisees, the boss can quickly become puffed with self-satisfaction.

Third, people in authority can make others do their personal bidding. Your demand outweighs their desire. This is an inevitable part of authority, but some seem to take a special pleasure in the thrill of power, in saying, "You have to do it because I say so."

Power can be an addictive drug. Some can only satisfy

their cravings with larger and larger doses. When addiction sets in, the exercise of power becomes its own reward, and ignoring the needs and wants of others becomes a way of life.

Unless the company is your own, the privileges, position, and power you hold are granted by somebody even further up the ladder than you. Therefore the ambitious supervisor worries "up," keeping an anxious eye on anything that might lead to another advancement, a bit more power, a few more people to direct.

The manager who worries up has little energy available to consider anyone but the individual who controls the next promotion. Not much is left for service. Indeed, rarely is thought given to service because those who worry up are focused on serving themselves.

The boss who accepts the role of the servant worries down. The encounter with the Gospel inevitably creates a concern for the needs and welfare of those below one on the organizational chart. The supervisor who worries down has an investment in helping the people he or she oversees do their jobs well and attain a sense of satisfaction with their work. He strives to help subordinates improve their own skills, and assists them in getting promotions and better jobs. Instead of putting all of his available energy into attaining into his own professional goals, this boss also works to help his workers reach their goals.

The Christian supervisor needs to worry down, exercising authority as a servant. But the supervisor usually has a boss of his or her own. So his or her two responsibilities, neither of which can be ignored, are to serve the Gospel and help the company run smoothly.

In fact, it often happens that the boss who worries down is actually a more effective manager than the eager self-promoter. And the notion of worrying up or down applies to all managers, whether or not Christian religion has a place in their lives.

Take a minute to recall some of the supervisors for whom you have worked. Can you remember any who were very busy worrying up? What was it like to work for them? How did you feel about your job and the organization you worked for?

Now see if you can recall a supervisor who worried down, who was concerned about you and about how you were doing. What was work like with such a boss? How did it make you feel about the job?

A big part of employee productivity is tied up in how people feel about the boss. These feelings affect their attitude towards work. People need to feel that their contributions are valued. A manager who worries up makes the people he supervises feel insignificant and unimportant. The message communicated is "Work hard so I can look good." A boss who doesn't care about the welfare of those he supervises shouldn't be surprised if they aren't too eager to help him get a bigger desk and more people to push around.

On the other hand, the manager who worries down, who seeks to serve, often generates enthusiasm and loyalty amongst the staff. If the boss cares about you as a person, you come to care about the boss. Loyalty cannot be purchased; it can only be earned. The boss can pay people enough to get them to stay, but money alone won't make them feel good about their jobs.

Nobody expects a job to be a party. Everybody knows that there is work to be done, and it is the supervisor's job to keep the work moving. The business or the agency will only survive if the job is done right.

The principal of a school is responsible for creating an atmosphere where teachers can teach. That means making sure that the staff is large enough, that the instructors have the materials they need, and that the bureaucratic craziness of the school system doesn't intrude too much on the teaching day. The principal who accomplishes these things serves his teachers and their students. The school is a better learning environment because of his efforts. The principal who worries up is rarely at the school building. He is too busy going to committee meetings, and worrying about being seen by people who might

142

control the next promotion. From the point of view of the school system, to say nothing of the teachers and students, the principal who worries down is a better manager.

Similarly, the boss has to be sure that individuals do their jobs. The manager who tolerates laziness or ineptitude on the part of one employee hurts all the others who must work harder to make up for that worker's incompetence. Those busy worrying up may not even notice that one or two poor employees are eroding the motivation of the rest of the staff.

Sometimes concern for one's employees means taking an individual to task for failing to produce. This may sound like an uncaring thing to do, but it can often be the greatest possible act of service both to that employee and to the other workers. If the boss communicates concern and willingness to help—to serve—along with the complaints, the message will be much easier for the worker to hear. Most people want to do a good job, and letting them know about the problems usually leads to improvement.

The usual response to the problem employee is counseling followed by threat and punishment. This entire procedure is almost certain to create resentment and fear. Supervisors sometimes try to avoid confronting problem workers altogether because they often suffer more pain and discomfort than the employee on the receiving end. It is the supervisor's job to deal with the unproductive employee, but the usual sequence of escalating threat and punishment leads to apathy, hostility, reduced output, and strained interpersonal relationships in the work place. No wonder many supervisors prefer to look the other way.

More caring and serving alternatives are available. In 1985 an article appeared in the *Harvard Business Review*, titled "Discipline Without Punishment—Why and How You Should Implement a Nonpunitive Approach to Discipline." The *Harvard Business Review* is not a theological quarterly. It is a matter-of-fact capitalist journal published for the ambitious and successful. The remarkable thing about this carefully documented article was its consistency with the vision of authority as service.

In the system they describe, the manager's primary goal is to gain the employee's agreement to solve the problem at hand. The first step is a private meeting with the employee to discuss the problem. Instead of issuing a threat—"Straighten up or else!"—the manager reminds the employee of his responsibility to meet reasonable company standards of performance and behavior. Typically, a note is made of the conversation, but it is kept in a working file rather than in the employee's company file. That way, if the problem is solved no punitive notes are stored where they may come back to haunt an employee who cooperated.

If the problem isn't solved, the second step is a written reminder. Again, there is a serious private conversation, but no threats. The manager reviews the rules, the sound business reasons for those rules, and discusses the employee's continuing problems. The employee's commitment to solve the problem is gained, and a plan is worked out. A written memo of intent is dictated and placed in the employee's file.

If the problem continues, in spite of these efforts and the employee's expressed intent to improve, the manager places the employee on a one-day paid "decision-making leave." The company pays the employee for a day off to think about the problem. This demonstrates the organization's desire to retain the employee. However, this step also makes it very clear that continued employment depends on the individual's decision to solve the problem and live up to the commitment. The employee is instructed to return on the day after the leave with a decision either to stay and change or to quit and find work elsewhere. If his decision is to stay, a plan is developed and commited to paper along with a statement that failure to meet its expectations will lead to termination.

This is a service-oriented model of discipline—the focus is always on helping the employee improve his or her performance. There are no threats, and the decision always lies with the employee. It is also a remarkable example of the practicality of worrying down. The authors of the article list company after company which have adopted this approach with positive results. They document reductions in turnover in a state department of mental health, fewer disciplinary incidents in a major manufacturing company, fewer grievances in a unionized telephone company, and reduced sick leave in a large utility. This is not just a "nice" idea as each of these results indicates major savings in real dollars.

The ultimate test for the Christian is not the balance sheet but the Gospel vision. If the Roman general's option of killing one problem employee in ten were legal and effective it would still not be acceptable for the Christian supervisor. However, the example of nonpunitive discipline shows that respecting and caring about the employee can produce practical results. One can follow Jesus and be an effective supervisor as well.

It is important to assess your usual direction of concern. Nobody worries exclusively up or down, but people tend to look in one direction more frequently. If you are in a managerial position it is important to know where you are placing the most attention. Answering the following questions may provide some clues.

When you are experiencing tension with someone you supervise, do you find yourself more worried about the employee's career needs or your own supervisor's reactions to what you are doing?

Whose long-term goals do you know more about: the five people you supervise or the two people who supervise you?

Whose wedding are you more likely to attend: the daughter of your boss, or the son of one of the women you supervise?

Would you rather talk with your boss about your goals for the next year or with one of your employees about his hopes and plans? When was the last time you sat down with someone you supervise and asked him what he wanted to be doing in ten years?

What concrete efforts have you made to help your supervisees gain new skills and abilities?

No single question or answer will provide you with the total picture. Service is not a single act. It is a way of living. However, careful attention to your pattern of concerns in your supervisory situation will almost certainly help you notice opportunities for service.

The exercise of authority, being the boss, is an important part of life in the working world. Jesus calls forth a response of loving service. He made Himself the servant of all, and He commands you to follow His example especially when you are in charge.

The greatest among you must be your servant. Anyone who exalts himself will be humbled and anyone who humbles himself will be exalted. (Matthew 23:11)

13

Your Work and
the Wider World

U P UNTIL NOW, IN DEALING WITH YOUR JOB AND your faith, the focus has been primarily on the business or bureaucratic community where you spend your working day. However, ours is a large and interconnected society. There are immense social problems experienced on a national or even a planetary scale, which can seem very distant from your employment. But the followers of Jesus are called to strive for peace and justice, for Koinonia and Shalom, beyond the boundaries of their small circle of friends and acquaintances.

The world is so big that it tends to make one feel powerless and insignificant. Americans share a cultural memory of a simpler time when towns were smaller and people knew one another. One would recognize the banker in the barber shop and run into friends and neighbors downtown. Now, instead of chatting with the corner grocer about neighborhood events, most Americans zip through supermarket checkout stands where the laser registers the prices and the computer prints the bill. The cashier is sure to say, "Thank you for shopping at

Ranco—have a nice day," but both the customers and the clerk know that they have not really communicated. The TV announces the news from Washington and Beirut, but few people even know the name of their local city council representative, let alone that of an official in the federal government.

An employee of a big company or a governmental agency can feel like an oarsman in a galley. Every one is working hard, and the boat is moving forward, but all that he can see is the back of the man on the next bench. He can only hope, and it is an act of faith, that the captain has a good map and knows how to navigate.

Somebody has to face the big problems, the major injustices that cause anguish in the world. But surely that person has to be someone with more power or more influence than you. The politicians, the wealthy, even today's rock stars, may be able to really make a difference. Our world is in trouble and sometimes it feels like time is running out.

"I'm not good enough," "I'm not powerful enough," "I'm not smart enough." All good excuses, but none good enough. Moses, Isaiah, John the Baptist, Peter, Paul, Zebedee's sons, the Virgin Mary, Matthew, and Zaccheus all had reason to draw back, to decide that the challenge was too much, that they didn't have the necessary skills. But they accepted the call, standing up to the powerful forces of their own times.

And then there was Jesus. Jerusalem was not a tiny backwoods village. Modern archeological research indicates that in New Testament times Jerusalem was home to 80,000 permanent residents, and during Passover another 100,000 pilgrims would join the throngs in those tiny streets. Jesus walked into a city dominated by the army of a distant empire and under the effective social control of His sworn enemies, the Scribes, Saduccees, and Pharisees. His best friends all tried to deter Him because they suspected what awaited Him there. And yet He went into Jerusalem fully aware of the powers He faced.

148

Jesus went to Jerusalem and was crucified there. He was arrested and murdered by the powers of empire, established religion, and fear. His success came only after the most visible kind of failure. The Resurrection was God's highest act of affirmation that the goodness of Christ is stronger than the evil in the world.

Christian moral life begins and ends with the call to follow Jesus, a man who stood up to the most frightening powers of His day. Early Christians followed His path, forming a church whose force of witness could not be overcome by centuries of fierce Imperial persecution. "I do not accept the empire of this world," said one Christian from Scillium in 180 A.D. He was martyred with his companions, yet the church persisted. The bishops of Rome, Antioch, and Jerusalem were all killed in the persecution under Emperor Decius (249–251 A.D.) and still the church followed Jesus.

The path of Jesus is not the Yellow Brick Road to the Emerald City; it leads to the cross and beyond. In our country, Christians are no longer physically persecuted for their faith. Still, there are powerful forces working to undermine humanity and to destroy the values of life. If you choose to follow Jesus, you may meet them face to face.

These forces have powerful allies. Huge corporations, giant industries, and massive political machines are devoted to maintaining the status quo. Much of what troubles the earth is beyond the control of any individual, group, or even any single nation. And yet Jesus calls you to exert your force in opposition to structural evil. Each day on the job you face numerous decisions, and every one of them is an opportunity to take your part in breaking down the patterns of selfishness, injustice, and fear.

The Consumer Society

American society is driven by the overriding goal to increase purchasing power—buy as much as you can. The more goods bought, the more services purchased, the happier the consumer. No wonder the bumper sticker reads, HE WHO DIES WITH THE MOST TOYS WINS.

People really want more than material possessions. They want to be happy, loved, valued, and seen as worthwhile. Advertisers promise to fill the deepest hungers of the human heart—love, intimacy, happiness, peace of mind—with possessions. Products are wrapped up in promises cleverly packaged in thirty-second ads. On the screen, a professional man and woman sip coffee and play chess in their lovely home. They have this time together because they bank by mail. The unspoken promise is, "Bank with us and you will have intimate time together, even though you both have busy careers." Another ad shows throngs of happy people drinking in a bar after work, and every moment of the ad shouts out, "If you drink our beer, you will have lots of friends and never be an outsider again!" The promise is a fraud. Possessions don't bring happiness. You can use all the right detergents and still have an unhappy marriage.

There are greater problems than the dashing of individual hopes based on empty promises. First, the advertising agencies appear to have gained control of our desires. This is especially evident among the young. In a department store a thirteen-year-old girl announces to her mother that a certain shirt is unacceptable—"It doesn't even have an ad on TV!" Obviously the advertiser's control is not complete, and many products still fail to catch the fancy of the consumer. But Americans have built a business ethic around the notion that it is fair to manipulate the consumer.

Second, with the emphasis on consumption, the wealthy nations of the world have laid financial claim to all the world's resources, and they are exhausting them at a frightening rate. Our economy is based upon supplying immediate fulfillment to demand, so there is no motivation to wait, no reason to do anything but consume. This eager consumption adds to the maldistribution of all the world's goods, and not just gas and oil.

Mexico lacks sufficient water to grow corn and beans

for the hungry children in Mexico City, and yet the state has an adequate supply to irrigate the lettuce and celery grown for the dinner tables in Los Angeles and Terre Haute. Americans want green vegetables in the winter and can pay for them in cash. The Mexican government, desperate for dollars to service their foreign debts, sends water for crops for American salads instead of for Mexican tortillas. Our consumption affects the rest of the world.

Finally, the consumer society gives rise to a theological issue. If happiness equals the ability to buy and consume goods and services, then what is God's role in our lives? Is the sovereign God of Scripture, who alone is the source of happiness, today just a pale deity whose purpose is to bless and assure our prosperity? It is tempting to make God over into a congenial image rather than submit to His very real demands. Popular idolatry, the worship of a God promising material comfort, stands in direct opposition to the God of Scripture.

As you make your daily decisions at work remember that you have opportunities to challenge the ethic of blind consumerism.

The Rich Against the Poor

There are millions of Americans and billions in the world who will never experience the sort of happiness that comes from enjoying wealth. The immense gap between the rich and the poor appears to be growing ever wider. Even in our wealthy country choices must be made about allocating resources. At the present time federal health services, food programs, and job training efforts are being washed away in the necessary effort to balance the budget. And the poor are left with less and less comfort.

Those who accept the false theology of God as Guarantor of Prosperity understand why we are rich and they are poor. He loves us more. America is the "promised land," the city on the hill chosen by God and blessed with more riches than any other nation in history. The

151

poor must have done something to upset God. Why else would He be so solidly on our side?

In the twentieth century Americans are the rich. The record of Scripture shows that God has repeatedly taken sides in the conflict between the rich and the poor—and He stands with the poor every time.

The critical event of the Hebrew Scripture is the liberation of the Jews enslaved by the Egyptians. God set them on a land, and they established a kingdom. But they became accustomed to their prosperity, and God raised up the prophet Amos to convey the unwelcome message that they themselves had become exploiters and oppressors of the poor.

The rich trample the head of the poor into the dust of the earth. (Amos 2:7)

The cost of their oppression and idolatry was the destruction of the northern kingdom of Israel.

In the next century, God raised up other prophets to bring the same message to the southern kingdom of Judah. Isaiah, Jeremiah, and Micah reproved the people for the same sins.

Woe to the legislators of infamous laws,
to those who issue tyrannical decrees,
who refuse justice to the unfortunate
and cheat the poor among my people of their rights,
who make widows their prey
and rob the orphan.
What will you do on the day of punishment,
when, from far off, destruction comes?
To whom will you run for help?
Where will you leave your riches?
Nothing for it but to crouch with the captives
and to fall with the slain.
Yet his anger is not spent,
still his hand is raised to strike. (Isaiah 10:1–4)

Jesus announced His ministry by reading from Isaiah in the synagogue at Nazareth—"He has sent me to bring the good news to the poor, to proclaim liberty to captives, and to the blind new sight, to set the downtrodden free, to proclaim the Lord's year of favor." (Luke 4:18–19) It would be possible to hear this as a purely symbolic message, but Jesus then went out and spent the majority of His time with poor people. Most of his life was spent with the outcasts, the poor, the sinners, the disreputable people of His time.

Biblical teachings on property, wealth, and poverty are complex, but certain themes emerge upon examination. The Scripture holds that wealth often blinds people to God's will that justice be done for all. Rather than simply discuss it, a believer must actually make an effort to assure that justice is done. The starkest passage in the New Testament is Jesus' description of the judgment day. It is to be found in the twenty-fifth chapter of Matthew. Divine judgment will be based on whether a person fed the hungry, gave drink to the thirsty, clothed the naked, and visited those in prison. How might Jesus have given any greater force to His choice to stand with the poor?

When your work provides opportunities to help the world's poor, to make justice a reality, remember the call of Jesus.

The War Machine

This century has seen two world wars, countless lesser conflicts and the increasing willingness of nations to keep their own populations under control through ruthless military power. Communist states, rightist dictatorships, and nations of all stripes are ready to resort to military violence to solve their internal problems.

The development and sale of weapons is the twentieth century's chief growth industry. The amount of money spent on weapons in this country alone is staggering. It is not uncommon for the papers to carry stories about debates over the military budget. Ten billion dollars less here, ten billion dollars more there—all this money is but small change in the military budget. The dollars that go into weapons come from somewhere, and they could be spent for other things.

Nuclear weapons raise the danger of total annihilation. If even a fraction of the arms we already possess were used in a conflict, all of the cities in the warring countries would be destroyed. No Moscow, no Toledo, no Davenport, Iowa—those cities and the vast majority of their inhabitants would simply no longer exist.

We cannot fulfill the Gospel by evaporating people. Whatever your position on deterrence as a policy, however you understand the struggle between Communism and Capitalism, there can be no starker issue than the use of those weapons. Each of us must seek to assure that they remain forever silent.

As you make your choices at work remember that Jesus called us to live in peace with our neighbors.

Someone has to face the critical problems in the world. Someone has to stand up and oppose the forces of greed, fear, and destruction which erode our values and threaten to bring a sudden, tragic end to the human saga. Someone must have the courage to speak with God's prophetic voice. Perhaps God has only one messenger available in your corner of the world. Perhaps that messenger is you.

"I'm not sure enough, God" may be your answer. Jerusalem is still a large and frightening city, even if you know that the resurrection lies beyond the cross. But, there is a paradox in the Christian's relationship to the holy. The closer you come to God, the more you know that Paul wrote the truth, that the power of God is indeed greatest in the midst of your weakness. (2 Corinthians 12:7-10)

Though he lived more than twenty-seven centuries ago, Isaiah's words still speak to men and women in our time. Having grown close to God, he was deeply troubled by the condition of his society and very much aware of his own inadequacy. He knew that the problems were too

154

big for him. But one day Isaiah had a vision of the power and the absolute holiness of God. He heard the angels standing before God cry out to one another:

Holy, holy, holy is Yahweh Sabaoth.
His glory fills the whole earth. (Isaiah 6:3)

Isaiah was then filled with a sense of his own unworthiness before God. He said:

What a wretched state I am in! I am lost,
for I am a man of unclean lips
and I live among a people of unclean lips,
and my eyes have looked at the King, Yahweh
Sabaoth. (Isaiah 6:5)

God needed a messenger, a prophet, to carry His word to the people. He cleansed Isaiah with a live ember and questioned him:

Whom shall I send? Who will be our messenger?
(Isaiah 6:8)

Isaiah responded from the depths of his fear with the words that became the enduring attitude of his entire ministry.

Here I am, send me. (Isaiah 6:9)

The rest was not all joy and victory. Isaiah accepted the burden of speaking God's word to a people fallen into sin. He suffered intensely because he insisted that Israel's sole hope lay in trusting God. Jewish tradition has long held that he died a martyr under Manasseh. He never rescinded his initial response.

God includes each of us in His question: "Whom shall I send?" For we too are men and women of unclean lips who live among a people similarly unclean in the sight

155

of God. But we have also been cleansed by God and called by Him to go out among our own people.

What is it that God calls us to do? If the work we do is also a Christian mission to the world, what is the nature of that mission? Here Scripture provides a breathtaking perspective. We are to alter creation itself, the great problems and the small, the War Machine as much as the office politics. Paul laid the groundwork for this capacious view. Of Christ he wrote:

He is the image of the unseen God
and the first-born of all creation,
for in him were created
all things in heaven and on earth:
everything visible and everything invisible,
thrones, dominations, sovereignties, powers—
all things were created through him and for him.

Before anything was created, he existed,
and he holds all things in unity.
Now the church is his body,
he is its head.

As he is the Beginning,
he was first to be born from the dead,
so that he should be first in every way;
because God wanted all perfection
to be found in him
and all things to be reconciled through him and for
him,
everything in heaven and everything on earth,
when he made peace
by his death on the cross. (Colossians 1:15–20)

Human civilization, with all its terrible faults, is an extension of God's creative work. A contemporary prayer summarizes the teaching of the first chapters of Genesis. God brought forth the human race from the primal elements and "blessed us with memory, reason and skill."

He then "made us the rulers of creation." (Episcopal Book of Common Prayer, p. 370) If it is largely through our work that we exercise this God-given power, then it is also through our work that we turn away from God, betraying His trust and joining with the powers of the world. Our work itself must be brought under the redeeming love of Christ.

Though humanity has wandered far from God, God has expressed His desire for all to be reconciled through Christ. Important opportunities for participation in that reconciliation come through your work. Your choices are facets of the peace which flows from His death and resurrection.

The followers of Jesus are called upon to take part in God's work. Paul did not say that Christ was the only one born from the dead but that He was the *first*. Paul's image of all creation "groaning in one great act of giving birth" (Romans 8:22) is heady indeed. You are a part of this new birthing of creation, called to change the world, one decision at a time—starting on Monday.

Each of us can participate in Christ's mission of reconciling all creation to God. You can take part in His mighty work. Touched by grace and called upon as a follower of Christ, you walk with Him in the workplace and in every other place as well. The fruit of your labors together will be nothing less than the re-creation of the world.

"Here I am, send me."

Appendix

A Listing of the Parables of Jesus:

The wise and foolish builders, Matthew 7:24-27; Luke 6:47,49.
Two debtors, Luke 7:41-47.
The rich fool, Luke 12:16-21.
The servants waiting for their Lord, Luke 12:35-40.
The barren fig tree, Luke 13:6-9.
The sower, Matthew 13:3-9; Mark 4:1-9; Luke 8:5-8, 11-15.
The tares, Matthew 13:24-30, 36-43.
Seed growing secretly, Mark 4:26-29.
Mustard seed, Matthew 13:31,32; Mark 4:30-32, Luke 13:18,19.
Leaven, Matthew 13:33; Luke 13:20,21.
Hidden treasure, Matthew 13:44.
Pearl of great price, Matthew 13:45,46.
Drawnet, Matthew 13:47-50.
Unmerciful servant, Matthew 18:23-35.
Good Samaritan, Luke 10:30-37.
Friend at midnight, Luke 11:5-8.
Good shepherd, John 10:1-16.
Great supper, Luke 14:15-24.
Lost sheep, Matthew 18, 24-14; Luke 15:3-7.
Lost piece of money, Luke 15:8-10.
The prodigal and his brother, Luke 15:11-32.
The unjust steward, Luke 16:1-9.
Rich man and Lazarus, Luke 16:19-31.

Importunate widow, Luke 18:1–8.
Pharisee and publican, Luke 18:9–14.
Laborers in the vineyard, Matthew 20:1–16.
The pounds, Luke 19:11–27.
The two sons, Matthew 21:28–32.
Wicked husbandmen, Matthew 21:33–44; Mark 12:1–12;
   Luke 20:9–18.
Marriage of the king's son, Matthew 22:1–14.
Fig tree leafing, Matthew 24:32; Mark 13:28,29.
Man taking a far journey, Mark 13:34–37.
Ten virgins, Matthew 25:1–13.
Talents, Matthew 25:14–30.
The vine, John 15:1–5.

Source: Nave, Orville J. *Nave's Topical Bible: A Digest of the Holy Scriptures.* Moody Press, Chicago, 1970. (pp. 707–8)

About the Authors

William P. Mahedy is an Episcopal Campus Pastor at the University of California at San Diego and San Diego State University. He served as an Army chaplain in Vietnam and, working with the Veterans Administration, helped develop the design for the Vietnam Veterans Outreach Program. Drawing on his insights and experiences in counseling veterans and lecturing on the moral and religious dimensions of war, Rev. Mahedy wrote *Out of the Night: The Spiritual Journey of Vietnam Vets*. He lives in San Diego with his wife and two children.

Christopher Carstens, a clinical psychologist, received his doctorate from the University of Connecticut and has published several papers on behavioral therapy and treatment. He is also a sought-after speaker at both professional and Christian conferences and workshops.

Dr. Carstens lives in San Diego with his wife and two children. He is an active leader in his community and has published articles in several Catholic publications. With William Mahedy, he wrote *Right Here, Right Now: Spiritual Exercises for Busy Christians*.

Bring New Meaning
and Insight Into Your Life
with

BALLANTINE/
EPIPHANY BOOKS